CORPORATE FINANCE MANUAL

DETERMINING
COST OF CAPITAL

DETERMINING COST OF CAPITAL

THE KEY TO FIRM VALUE

Dr Hazel Johnson

FINANCIAL TIMES

PRENTICE HALL

PEARSON EDUCATION LIMITED

Head Office:
Edinburgh Gate
Harlow CM20 2JE
Tel: +44 (0)1279 623623
Fax: +44 (0)1279 431059

London Office:
128 Long Acre, London WC2E 9AN
Tel: +44 (0)171 447 2000
Fax: +44 (0)171 240 5771

First published in Great Britain in 1999

ISBN 0 273 63880 7

British Library Cataloguing in Publication Data
A CIP catalogue record for this book can be obtained
from the British Library.

1 3 5 7 9 10 8 6 4 2

Typeset by Northern Phototypesetting Co Ltd.
Printed and bound in Great Britain by
Redwood Books, Trowbridge, Wiltshire.

*The Publishers' policy is to use paper manufactured
from sustainable forests.*

ABOUT THE AUTHOR

Dr Hazel J. Johnson is Distinguished University Scholar at the University of Louisville and Professor of Finance (USA). Dr Johnson was formerly a member of the finance faculty of Georgetown University (Washington, DC, USA). She has authored more than 20 books in the areas of international finance and financial institutions. With publications in the USA, Europe, Latin America, and Asia, Dr Johnson's work has been translated into Japanese and Spanish. In addition, she has developed software systems for business practitioners in the areas of bank valuation, capital budgeting, cost of capital, and mergers and acquisitions. Dr Johnson has acted as a consultant to more than 50 major US financial institutions and a number of state and federal agencies.

In loving memory of Ida W. Kelly
and Lucille V. Johnson.

CONTENTS

FOREWORD

Making the right decision about major capital investments depends in large measure on the firm's cost of capital. An investment in property, equipment, or another company is advisable if the investment will earn the cost of capital. If the investment does not clear this hurdle rate, the value of the firm will decline. The correct assessment of the cost of capital is one of the most critical management decisions.

Determining Cost of Capital: The Key to Firm Value helps managers identify each source of capital and to differentiate these sources. Capital includes bank financing in the form of lines of credit, term loans, asset-based loans, and syndicated loans. Other sources of debt capital are medium-term notes, domestic bonds, and international bonds. Firms obtain equity capital by issuing preferred and common stock. The ultimate mix of these capital components will drive the firm's cost of capital. An increasingly important aspect of raising new capital is securitization of loans and trade receivables: that is, pooling financial assets and selling claims to the pool to investors. The book describes computing the cost of capital for every mix of debt and equity and for varying risk environments.

The *Cost of Capital Software Systems* which accompanies the book implements the concepts. With modules for debt, preferred stock, and common stock, the Excel based system permits the evaluation of cost of capital by a publicly-traded firm and by a privately-held company. Debt information for the firm is automatically analyzed to arrive at the after-tax cost of debt on a weighted basis. Cost of preferred equity is computed on the basis of parameters of the issue. Cost of common equity for a publicly-traded company is based on the most advanced approach – market parameters, government security returns, and the relative volatility of the company stock. For a privately-held company, cost of common equity is derived from comparable industries and the firm's debt-to-equity ratio. The system computes beta the measure of risk for common stock. In every case, the weighted average cost of capital is automatically computed.

Determining Cost of Capital: The Key to Firm Value answers critical questions:

- What are the factors that affect a firm's cost of capital in the case of each supplier of capital?
- How does a change in the cost of capital affect the selection of capital projects?
- How is risk and uncertainty incorporated into the cost of capital?

Both the book and the software system are designed to be a ready resource to support management efforts to maximize the value of the firm.

CHAPTER 1

WHAT IS CAPITAL?

Introduction

◾

Intermediate Debt

◾

Long-term Debt

◾

Equity Capital

◾

Public versus Private Placement

◾

Facilitating Growth of the Firm

INTRODUCTION

Capital is the lifeblood of a company – the source of long-term financing for the firm. While common equity is an integral part of corporate funding, it is increasingly being supplemented by other forms of capital.

ICI presents an intriguing example of the wide array of financing alternatives in raising capital.[1]

■ ■ ■

In May 1997, ICI announced the acquisition of Unilever's Specialty Chemicals business for $8 billion.

■ In the same month that the acquisition was announced, ICI obtained a five-year syndicated loan arranged by Goldman Sachs, HSBC, and SBC Warburg. The $8.5 billion was divided into a $4 billion revolving credit and $4.5 billion in an amortizing term loan. From the outset, the intention was to refinance the loans through asset sales and with publicly issued debt.[2]

■ Early in July 1997, ICI sold company divisions in the amount of $3.6 billion.

■ Also early in July, ICI raised $2 billion in commercial paper.[3]

■ Mid-July, ICI initiated a $4 billion medium-term-note (MTN) program lead by Deutsche Morgan Grenfell.
  – The first issue under the program was a $500 million five-year Eurobond, led by Deutsche Morgan Grenfell and Union Bank of Switzerland.
  – One week later, ICI raised £300 million in a ten-year Eurobond led by Barclays de Zoete Wedd (BZW) and NatWest Markets.

---

[1] ICI is an acronym for Imperial Chemical Industries PLC, London. ICI had $10.5 billion in sales in 1997 and generated $275 million in profits. The firm develops, manufactures, and markets petrochemicals, polymers, and industrial chemicals and also manufactures acrylics, paints, and industrial chemicals.

[2] Since ICI intended to refinance the loan with bonds, the banks negotiated for the ability to assign the loans. This gave the financial institutions the flexibility to sell part or all of the loans and then to participate in the underwritten bonds that were planned for future issuance.

[3] Although commercial paper is a short-term liability, companies often roll over commercial paper upon maturity, thus creating a source of longer-term finance.

- In early August, a £100 million private placement was issued in 18-month floating rate notes (FRNs), led by SBC Warburg.
- One week later, a $1.25 billion FRN was issued in three tranches of $500 million maturing in one year, $500 million in 15 months, and $250 million in 18 months, led by Deutsche Morgan Grenfell.
- In September, ICI issued $1.25 billion in Yankee bonds – $150 million maturing in five years, $750 million in seven years, and $250 million in ten years. Since Yankee bonds are issued in the United States by non-U.S. issuers, the lead manager was the US firm Goldman Sachs.
- The last piece of refinancing consisted of a 364-day revolving credit of £1.5 billion, arranged in October by NatWest Markets and Midland Bank.

■   ■   ■

In a few short months, ICI tapped syndicated bank financing, short-term financing by investors, Eurobond markets, the US bond market, and private placement financing.[4] All of these forms of financing are part of the potential capital of a firm. Indeed, the list of possible forms of capital includes:

Intermediate Debt
- Bank financing
  - Lines of credit
  - Term loans
  - Asset-based loans
  - Syndicated loans
- Commercial paper
- Medium-term notes.

---

[4] See "A Case Study in Capital Raising," by Jeremy Adams in *Corporate Finance*, December 1997,

Long-term Debt

- Domestic bonds
- International bonds
  - Eurobonds
  - Foreign bonds
  - Global bonds.

Equity Capital

- Preferred stock
- Common stock.

In those cases in which the capital is not raised through bank financing, an important decision is whether to issue through public or private placement. All of these factors will ultimately impact the firm's cost of capital.

INTERMEDIATE DEBT

Intermediate debt capital can be obtained primarily from bank financing, the rollover of short-term commercial paper, and/or through the issuance of medium-term notes.

Bank Financing

Bank financing can be obtained in many different forms. However, for comparative purposes, the following classifications are useful:

- lines of credit
- term loans
- asset-based loans
- commercial real estate loans
- syndicated loans.

Lines of Credit

A *working capital line of credit* is a pre-approved credit facility that enables a bank customer to borrow up to a specified maximum amount at any time during the relevant period of time, in most cases, one year. In this case, the bank and its client agree on the terms of the arrangement once each year. They mutually agree upon the maximum amount of credit that will be available, the interest rate, and the *commitment fee* – the rate charged to a bank customer for the unused portion of a line of credit. Interest is charged only on actual borrowings. The commitment fee (usually less than 1 percent per annum) is charged on the part of the credit line that the client does not use. The bank will commonly require the client to reduce borrowings to zero at least once a year in order to verify seasonality of the financing need, as appropriate. A variable-rate line of credit may be associated with a cap (maximum interest rate), a floor (minimum interest rate), or a collar (combination of a cap and a floor).

Revolving lines of credit may extend beyond one year, involving repayment over a period of years. If the purpose of the loan is acquisition of plant or equipment, funds are advanced in full, right away. If the need is related to higher anticipated permanent working capital needs, funds are advanced as needed.

Term Loans

A *term loan* extends beyond one year and up to 15 years, with the most common maturities falling between one and five years. This is the most common form of intermediate bank loan to commercial enterprises. It is appropriate to finance inventory, permanent working capital needs, or plant and equipment with term loans. The loan repayment schedule may require monthly, quarterly, semiannual, or annual payments. The loan rate will often float with either the bank's cost of funds, the interbank rate, London interbank offered rate (LIBOR), or the bank's prime rate. For example, if the loan is priced at "LIBOR plus 1," the interest rate is 1 percent over LIBOR. A variable-rate term loan also may be associated with a cap, a floor, or a collar.

Asset-based Loans

An *asset-based loan* is any loan that is secured by assets of the borrowing firm that are directly related to loan repayment. Loans based on inventory or accounts receivable are considered working capital asset-based loans. Accounts receivable provide the borrower a higher *borrowing base* (the amount a lender is willing to advance against the dollar value of collateral) because receivables are more liquid than inventory. In either case, the loan is repaid as inventory is sold or as receivables are collected.

Loans for leveraged buyouts (LBOs) are asset-based loans to investors who intend to purchase a firm, perhaps because the company has undervalued assets. Once the firm has been purchased, some of the undervalued assets are sold at prices closer to true value and the proceeds are used to repay the loan.

Commercial Real Estate Loans

Commercial real estate loans are used to purchase or construct apartment buildings, office buildings, shopping centers, and other facilities. They fall into three general categories:

- commercial mortgage loans
- zero-coupon mortgages
- construction and land development loans.

The **commercial mortgage loan** is secured by commercial real estate such as an office building, apartment building, or shopping mall and is a highly customized arrangement over a 20- to 40-year term. While the loan rate for most commercial mortgages floats based on an index, some are arranged with a fixed rate.

A **zero-coupon mortgage** is a commercial mortgage in which there are no payments of interest or principal during the term of the loan. Instead, interest accrues at either a fixed or variable rate and is added to the principal of the loan. The rationale for such a loan is that the borrower can finance the project with a small cash flow and the appreciation in property value will pay off the mortgage at maturity.

Construction and land development loans are used to complete commercial real estate projects and are a form of interim financing. Funds are advanced to the borrower at specific stages of project completion. These progress payments will be made, for example, when a certain percentage of the building has been leased to third parties (tenants). Upon completion, the project is funded by permanent mortgage financing from which the construction and land development loan is repaid. The party providing the permanent financing is referred to as a take-out lender.

If the project is an office building or retail facility, an adequate number of tenants is critical to its success. If the project is a development of residential units, ultimate sales are the key. The bank faces maximum exposure to loan loss when the real estate developer has not pre-leased or pre-sold the project and there is no take-out commitment.

Syndicated Loans

A *syndicated loan* differs from a conventional commercial loan in that several banks provide credit instead of one institution. The model for the syndicated loan in Euromarkets has been the multi-bank, floating-rate loan that was developed and refined in the USA. The vehicle has been particularly useful for governments and major corporations. The reasons for its development were:

- increasingly larger individual loans;
- a desire by international bankers to diversify risk;
- fee income potential for management of the loan;
- favorable public visibility for participating banks;
- enhanced working relationships with other banks.

The interest rate associated with a Euromarket syndicated loan is usually quoted as a spread over LIBOR. A lead bank or syndicate manager negotiates this interest rate and all other terms and conditions of the loan with the borrower, documenting them in the loan agreement. Participating banks then each purchase some portion of the total loan.

London has historically served as the primary location for international loan syndications. Other sites that have developed include Singapore, Hong Kong, Bahrain, Luxembourg, and the Caribbean.

The participating banks will expect that the normal, necessary conditions of prudent lending be satisfied. That is, the borrower should be creditworthy, the interest rate competitive, and appropriate restrictive covenants incorporated into the loan agreement. In addition, participating banks expect the lead manager to perform in a way that is consistent with their own financial interests. Ultimately, however, participating banks accept the full credit risk of the borrower for their respective parts of the loan. The syndication process enables regional banks to take part in large international transactions that might, otherwise, be unavailable to them.

Commercial Paper

Commercial paper is issued by corporations as unsecured promissory notes, with an original maturity of 270 days or less, in large denominations, primarily by the most creditworthy firms. Technically, commercial paper is not capital because it has an original maturity of less than one year. However, commercial paper is most often rolled over at maturity – creating an intermediate-term form of financing.

Commercial paper is a convenient way to raise short-term funds in the USA because registration with the US Securities and Exchange Commission (SEC) is not necessary, unlike public issuance of other securities. In order to be exempt from SEC registration, the issue must have an original maturity of 270 days or less and be intended for current transactions. The most common maturities of commercial paper are between 20 and 45 days. Most commercial paper is issued on a discounted basis.[5]

Because commercial paper is unsecured, the credit rating of the issuing company is a critical factor in the marketability of the issues. Three credit-rating firms rate most issues – Standard & Poor's Corporation (S&P), Moody's Investors Service, and Fitch Investor Service. S&P designates investment grade (high-quality) commercial paper as A-1 (highest investment grade), A-2 (high investment grade), and A-3 (good investment grade). Moody's comparable ratings are P-1, P-2, and P-3, while Fitch rates better-quality paper F-1, F-2, or F-3. Over 70 percent of the commercial paper rated by these firms receives the highest rating and 98 percent receives the highest two ratings, which gives some measure of the importance of creditworthiness for successful marketing.

Banks play an important role in these high average ratings. In most instances, issuing firms have backup lines of credit that cover 100 percent of the issue. When the credit of the issuing firm does not justify one of the top ratings, the firm may obtain a letter of credit from a bank with a top credit rating.[6] A letter of credit that backs the commercial paper, in effect, substitutes the credit rating of the bank for the credit rating of the issuer. This is called a *support arrangement* and the commercial paper is called "commercial paper supported by letter of credit" or a "documented discount note." In addition to banks, supporting institutions are insurance companies and parent companies (in the case of subsidiaries).

The secondary market for commercial paper is not as active as for other short-term instruments such as short-term government securities or

---

[5] *Discounted basis* means that commercial paper is issued at a price less than its maturity value and pays no interest between date of issuance and date of maturity. The difference between the issue price and the maturity value is interest earned by the investor. If the commercial paper is sold on the secondary market prior to maturity – only occasionally done – interest is the difference between the market price and the maturity value.

[6] A *letter of credit* is a letter issued by a bank or other financial institution indicating that a firm has arranged to obtain financing up to a specified amount.

negotiable bank CDs.[7] Dealers and direct issuers will redeem an issue prior to maturity if the investor is in dire need of funds, but early redemption is not encouraged. Of course, given that original maturities are so short, early redemption is generally not necessary.

Eurocommercial paper is issued by firms in markets outside their domestic markets. This instrument is one of the more recent to develop in Euromarkets. Throughout the 1970s and early 1980s, both US and foreign borrowers relied heavily on the US commercial paper market. Even though the first issue of Eurocommercial paper was in 1970 by an American firm, this form of financing did not gain widespread acceptance until the mid-1980s. The market has become more appealing as an alternative to short-term bank loans through arrangements that permit an issuer to request immediate sale of the paper or that allow a securities dealer to solicit an issue when the timing is most advantageous. Advances in communications technology have made precise timing of Eurocommercial paper issues possible. In addition, commercial paper interest rates compare favorably with other sources of financing.

Medium-term Notes

Euronotes are similar to Eurocommercial paper except that they include an additional agreement, a Euronote facility by an underwriter, promising that the underwriter will place the issuer's notes, when issued, for a specified period of time. This makes a Euronote facility a medium-term credit arrangement, often referred to as a *Euro medium-term note* (EMTN). For a number of reasons, this form of financing has become popular. High-quality credits have embraced the EMTN structure enthusiastically because it favors borrowers that regularly tap the market and is a flexible method of financing. EMTNs require a standard form of documentation

---

[7] A *negotiable CD* is a certificate of deposit issued by a bank or thrift institution that can be sold to other investors up to the date of maturity. Negotiable CDs are sold in $100,000 minimum amounts, but usually in round lots of $1 million.

---

that has been accepted by many investors and issuers. This standardization represents a significant cost saving for the borrowers and enables borrowers to move quickly to float issues when market conditions are favorable.

Less seasoned borrowers find the EMTN market attractive, as well. EMTNs enable borrowers to evaluate the reception of the Euromarket for their paper (debt) before embarking on a full-fledged Eurobond issue. Furthermore, an initial issue of EMTNs does not lock in the borrower to relatively high interest rates. After the issuer's credit standing strengthens, subsequent notes may be issued at lower rates.

Borrowers that have had past credit problems find the instruments a good way to reintroduce their names to international capital markets, frequently through private placements with a group of sympathetic investors.[8]

From the investors' perspective, one negative aspect of EMTNs is that they are not as liquid as conventional Eurobonds in the secondary market. However, a number of issuers – anxious to maintain the market – have bought back EMTN issues that became illiquid.

The EMTN market should continue its strong growth because it is being expanded beyond the plain vanilla note format. Structured EMTNs – that is, those that are linked to derivatives – once represented 28 percent of the total outstanding, but now amount to 75 percent of the outstanding issues. Many structures include *hedges on foreign-currency exposure* – once requested only by Japanese investors, but now being aggressively sought by European investors. When interest rates fall in Europe, *inverse floaters* and *duration-enhanced structures* are particularly popular.

- **Inverse floaters** have an interest rate that increases when the specified index (often LIBOR) decreases and vice versa.
- **Duration-enhanced notes** involve a swap that has been leveraged in

---

[8] A private placement is not issued to the general public, but to a small group of investors (35 or less) who are considered to have knowledge of the markets, usually institutional investors. In the USA, registration with the SEC is not required.

---

order to increase the interest rate sensitivity to a level that is more common in long-dated bonds.

With these enhancements, the EMTN market is projected to increase from the approximately 300 programs that are currently established to 700 – a conservative estimate.

1

LONG-TERM DEBT

Long-term debt enables the issuer to obtain financing for periods in excess of ten years and, in some cases, up to 20 years. This form of debt financing is composed primarily of *bonds* which are contractual liabilities that obligate the issuer to pay a specified amount (the par, face, or maturity value) at a given date in the future (the maturity date), generally with periodic interest payments in the interim at a fixed rate (the coupon rate).

Some bonds have a *call provision* which entitles the issuer to retire the bond before maturity. Because a call is exercisable at the discretion of the issuer and deprives the investor of anticipated income, a *call premium* (the excess of the call price over par value) is often payable to the investor upon call. This is particularly true if the issuer calls the bond because current interest rates are significantly below the bond's coupon rate. If the issuer calls the bond in order to comply with sinking fund requirements (gradual bond retirement), the call premium is generally much lower. In any event, call premiums decline as the maturity date of the bond approaches. Often, bonds may not be called for several years after issuance; this period of time is referred to as *call protection*.

Some bonds do not pay periodic interest but are discounted in much the same way as commercial paper. These bonds are called *zero coupon bonds*. Other bonds carry a coupon rate that changes with market interest rates. These *variable rate bonds* serve to protect investors from adverse bond price changes, but they also prevent investors from locking in high rates of interest for extended periods of time.

Bondholder rights and bond issuer responsibilities are included in the *indenture*. The indenture is a written agreement specifying the terms and conditions for a particular bond and states the form of the bond, interest to be paid, interest payment dates, maturity date, call provisions (as applicable), and any other condition that protects the rights of the bond-holders (restrictive covenants).

Domestic Bonds

There is a wide array of domestic corporate bond structures:

- mortgage bonds
- equipment trust certificates
- debentures
- subordinated debentures.

In some cases, bonds allow conversion into common stock and others include warrants that can be exercised to buy common stock.

Firms issue *mortgage bonds* to finance specific projects. Once built or placed in operation, the project becomes collateral for the bond issue, making the issue *secured* debt. Power utility companies are frequent issuers of mortgage bonds. Should the issuer default on the obligation, bondholders may legally take title to the project (collateral) in order to satisfy the debt.

Tangible property also collateralizes *equipment trust certificates*. In this case, the property is specific pieces of large equipment, usually the rolling stock of railroads (railcars) and airplanes. The collateral of equipment trust certificates may be more readily marketable than that of mortgage bonds in the event of a bond default.

Debentures are long-term liabilities that are supported not by collateral but only by the general creditworthiness of the issuer. For this reason, they are riskier from an investor's perspective. In case of bankruptcy, while the collateral behind mortgage bonds and equipment trust certificates can be sold to satisfy the obligations of the secured debt, holders of debentures are general creditors of the firm; they receive distributions only after the secured creditors have been paid.

Subordinated debentures are also unsecured, but they are junior in rights to debentures. In the event of liquidation, subordinated debenture holders receive a cash distribution only after more senior debt (both secured and unsecured) has been repaid. If debentures are subordinated to bank loans, for example, bank loans must be completely satisfied in a liquidation before the subordinated debenture holders receive any of the proceeds from asset sales.

Corporate bonds may sometimes be exchanged for other securities. *Convertible bonds* may be exchanged for a specific number of shares of common stock of the issuing firm. An investor will not elect to surrender the bond and convert, however, unless the market value of the stock to which the investor is entitled exceeds the market value of the bond. In the case of widely traded issues, the price of the bond fluctuates to keep its market value roughly equivalent to the value of the stock into which it may be converted. However, regardless of the market value of the stock, the owner of a convertible bond will never be entitled to less than the principal and interest payments of the bond.

Bonds are sometimes issued with *stock warrants* attached. Warrants are options to purchase common stock at a specified price up to a specified date. Should the bondholder decide to exercise the option and purchase stock, it is not necessary to surrender the underlying bond. Again, bond-holders will exercise their warrants only if the market value of the stock exceeds the specified (exercise) price of the warrant.

International Bonds

Generally, international bonds are either *Eurobonds* or *foreign bonds*. Recently, the advent of *global bonds* has extended the scope of international bond markets.

Eurobonds

Eurobonds are issued by parties outside their domestic capital markets, underwritten by an international investment banking syndicate, placed in at least two countries, and, perhaps, issued in more than one currency. The firms that underwrite Eurobonds generally maintain offices in New York, London, Tokyo, and other Euromarket centers. An international underwriting syndicate and multinational placement distinguish Eurobonds from other international issues.

Eurobond issuer and investor need not *necessarily* be in different countries. For example, a US firm may issue a Eurobond and sell part of it to a US insurance company while also selling to investors in other countries.

Foreign Bonds

In the case of *foreign bonds*, the country of origin of the issuer is *not* the same as that of the investor. Foreign bonds are issued by entities outside their own domestic capital markets in a foreign market, underwritten by a firm that is domestic to that foreign market, usually denominated in the currency of the market in which they are issued, but occasionally denominated in another currency.

Foreign bonds are sometimes referred to as *traditional* international bonds because they existed long before Eurobonds. Foreign bonds sometimes have specific names depending on the country of issue. Examples of these names are shown in Figure 1.1.

FIGURE 1.1

Foreign Bonds and Their Names

Country	Name of foreign bond
USA	Yankee bond
UK	Bulldog bond
Japan	Samurai bond
Spain	Matador bond
Portugal	Navigator bond
Asia (outside Japan)	Dragon bond

A gradual decline in the relative importance of the US dollar in international bond markets is linked to several factors. Uncertainties about the stability of the value of the dollar, over time, have contributed to the use of other currencies. Liberalization of regulations in the UK, Japan, Germany, and France have made international bond issuance easier. Lastly, the popularity of currency swaps has made it possible to issue Eurobonds in one currency and swap the proceeds for another currency.

Global Bonds

Global bonds are one of the newest variants of international bonds, with one *tranche* (portion of the total issue) placed in the Eurobond market and a second placed in the USA by a nonresident – a Yankee bond. The Yankee bond tranche is issued under full SEC registration. Issuers benefit because this form of security expands the number of investors that hold the bonds. Issuers also benefit from the increased liquidity of the bonds, sometimes lowering their cost of funds by as much as 0.20 percent or 20 basis points.

The market for global bonds involves investors that are financially sophisticated. Issuers in this market must be able to establish creditability on an international basis, particularly in Europe and the USA.

The growth of global bonds is indicative of the general trend of new products in the provision of cross-border financial services. This trend is supported by derivatives such as currency swaps that permit issuers to denominate their obligations in one currency but swap into another currency. Technology has also played an important role because it has facilitated trading of global bonds after issuance, that is, in the secondary market.

EQUITY CAPITAL

Equity capital is corporate stock and represents an ownership interest in the firm. Equity is recorded as the difference between a firm's assets and liabilities. Furthermore, the claim represented by an equity security does not mature, that is, is a perpetual claim on the issuer. Corporate stock takes two forms:

- preferred stock
- common stock.

The stock holder, whether a common stock holder or a preferred stock holder, has a claim on the issuing firm that has a lower priority than that of any debt holder.

Preferred Stock

Preferred stock is a hybrid instrument that represents an equity interest but pays a fixed dividend (just as a bond pays a fixed interest payment).[9] Often preferred stock is *cumulative*, that is, all preferred dividends (unpaid in the past and currently due) must be paid before common shareholders may receive any dividend payments. Because the dividend is fixed, a preferred stock holder is entitled to a perpetual stream of level cash flows. An alternative term used to describe this type of equity is *preference stock*.

The vast majority of preferred stock that is issued follows the model of indefinite life and fixed dividend payments. However, there are exceptions, the most common of which are:

- limited life preferred stock with a "maturity date" of at least 25 years after the date of issuance;
- money market preferred stock with a floating dividend rate that changes every 49 days – this structure is intended to ensure that the stock trades at or near par value at all times;
- adjustable rate preferred stock which pays dividends on a quarterly basis and adjusts the amounts of dividends with the same frequency – while adjustable rate issues do not mature, they may be callable at the option of the issuer.

---

[9] Dividends are periodic cash flows paid to owners of corporate stock (frequently paid on a quarterly basis).

Preferred stock may also be structured to be convertible into common stock.

Preferred stock holders usually have no voting rights. Yet preferred issues are often associated with the right to elect a minority of the company's board, if a preferred dividend is passed, that is, not paid. Companies have the right to pass a preferred stock dividend, but rarely do so. Nonpayment of preferred dividends means that common dividends may not be paid, and makes it difficult for the company to raise funds by selling bonds – and extremely difficult to sell more preferred or common stock.

Common Stock

Common stock is an equity interest with dividend payments that are not fixed and that vary, usually increasing over time. In the event of liquidation, common shareholders have the lowest priority in terms of any cash distribution.[10] Because of this, owners of common stock have what is called a *residual* claim on the firm.

Domestic Common Stock

The common shareholders control the firm in that they elect the firm's directors. In turn, the directors elect the officers who manage the company. In small- and medium-sized firms, the major shareholders usually hold the positions of president and chair of the board of directors. In large firms, managers may not have controlling shares. Common shares may be issued in different classes, for example, Class A and Class B. The names of the classes have no special meaning, but the function of each class does. For example, Class A may refer to the shares owned by the founders of a firm, which are the voting shares, but receive no dividends for some period of time. Class B shares may be issued to the public and have no

---

[10] After subordinated debentures, the next priority is preferred stock. After preferred stock claims are satisfied, common stock cash distributions are made.

voting rights for a specified period of time, but receive regular dividends. Such a structure enables the firm to raise capital, the investors to receive predictable income, while the founders retain control.

Euroequities

Euroequities are stocks offered outside the issuer's domestic capital market in one or more foreign markets and underwritten by an international syndicate. Issuing equities outside the home country market is not a new practice; firms have often floated stock issues in other countries when their domestic market was too small to absorb a large issue. Firms have issued stock in London or other major capital markets.

Euroequities are differentiated from these more traditional international issues by the nature of the underwriting syndicate. The same network of investment firms and banks that has been active in the Eurobond market now also underwrites equity issues. To the extent that an issue or a portion of an issue is offered through such an international syndicate, it is a Euroequity issue. As is true with other Euromarkets, the home of the Euroequity market is London.

Frequently, large corporations issue two or more *tranches*, that is, groups of identical or similar securities, each offered under slightly different terms and conditions or being distributed in different ways. A multinational firm may offer domestic and international tranches, for example, with the international tranche distributed through a Euromarket syndicate, thereby qualifying as a Euroequity.

The best candidates for this form of distribution are firms that have an international product market, so that name recognition abroad will help ensure adequate investor interest. International placement helps issuing firms receive a price that is determined by worldwide market conditions and to diversify across a wider shareholder base.

PUBLIC VERSUS PRIVATE PLACEMENT

A *public offering* of securities is intended for sale to the general public. On the other hand, a *private placement* is sold to a small group of investors. Any public offering of securities must be registered with the appropriate national regulatory body in the country of issue. In addition, public issues must comply with local securities laws (state or provincial).

Generally, the requirements of the national regulatory body are the primary challenge in a public offering. If a firm that has already issued public securities enters the primary market (market for new issues), that offering is referred to as a *public offering*. On the other hand, if the firm has never issued securities to the public at large, the offering is referred to as an *initial public offering*. There are often stringent disclosure requirements on the issuer in both a public offering and initial public offering. The objective of the disclosure requirements is to ensure that all potential investors have adequate information to make an informed decision. The only exceptions to this general rule are those securities with short initial maturities (commercial paper) or securities offered for *private placement*.

Private Placements in the USA

Because private placements bypass the registration process, they are faster and more flexible. In the USA, for example, the ability to offer a private placement is based on the Securities Act of 1933. In this legislation, the formal requirements for registration with the Securities Exchange Commission (SEC) were established. Within the same legislation, it was made clear that the investors who could be considered knowledgeable and sophisticated need not be protected. In a private placement, the responsibility for obtaining adequate information prior to investment is shifted to investors. In fact, the terms of a private placement are negotiated between the issuer and the investor. This is in contrast to the public offering in which the deal is structured and offered to the public after decisions about deal structure have been made.

While there is no limit on the number of potential investors that may be approached in the USA to purchase a private placement (since the 1982 issuance of Regulation D), the SEC does require that these investors be able to demonstrate both the capacity and intent to hold the securities for an extended period of time. The investors that can make such commitments and demonstrate such capacity and intent are large financial institutions such as insurance companies, private pension funds, and public pension funds. The investors' intent to hold the privately placed securities is documented in an *investment letter*, also called a *letter of intent*.

After two years, these restricted securities can be sold to the public in a limited fashion under *SEC Rule 144*. If the owner has no management or major ownership interests in the company, restricted securities may be sold to the public without full registration if:

- the securities have been owned and fully paid for at least two years, or upon the death of the owner;
- current financial information is made available to the buyer (companies that file annual and quarterly reports with the SEC satisfy this requirement);
- the seller files Form 144, "Notice of Proposed Sale of Securities," with the SEC no later than the first day of the sale (the filing is effective for 90 days; if the seller wishes to extend the selling period or sell additional securities, a new Form 144 is required).

Under Rule 144, the sale of the restricted securities may not be advertised. Also, if restricted stocks were owned for between two and three years, the volume sold is limited to the greater of (1) 1 percent of all outstanding shares or (2) the average weekly trading volume of all shares for the proceeding four weeks. On the other hand, if the restricted shares have been owned for three years or more, no volume restrictions apply to non-insider sellers of the stock (those with no management or major ownership interests).

For the issuer, the advantage of a private placement is that the cost associated with a public offering may be reduced or avoided – that is, flotation costs (underwriting spread and out-of-pocket expenses) and administrative costs of managing the issue. Also, issuers may place their securities more quickly than is possible with a public placement. In addition, deals can be customized to meet the needs of both the issuer and the investor without concerns for features that would make the securities more acceptable to a wider investor pool. Private placements may also be advisable if the firm has a limited credit history, that is, unrated or less than investment grade.

The typical structure of a private placement will involve 35 or fewer investors, all of whom sign the investment letter. While the investment letter states that securities will not be resold for a specific period of time – usually two years – the issue may be associated with a provision that permits registration with the SEC at a later time to improve its marketability. In addition, *Rule 144A* makes it possible for privately held securities to be resold to institutional investors without registration with the SEC.

Global Private Placements

In the early 1990s, J. P. Morgan & Company introduced *global private placements* in the fixed-income (bond) market. Potentially, this instrument could allow viable borrowers from almost any country to finance their enterprises through simultaneous placements in Europe, Japan, and the USA.

Straight bond deals became popular in Europe in the late 1980s after the US junk (or high-yield) bond market suffered major reverses. European investors are looking for good-quality credits that will yield a reasonable rate of return. In the private placement market, borrowers can convey their circumstances to individual investors in ways that are not possible in a public market. This improved information flow allows borrowers to more efficiently price their issues and reduce the cost of borrowing.

Until 1993, most of the demand for private placement came from Japanese leasing companies looking for subordinated bank debt. When this demand began to wane because of difficult conditions in the Japanese financial markets, investment bankers began to target investors in other regions of Asia, in Europe, and in the USA. It is the addition of the US investor in these deals that has given the market its biggest boost. Private placements that are structured with Rule 144A documentation have been used for some time (see section above on *Private placement in the USA*) by issuers from emerging markets. Rule 144A documentation represents only a modest increase in the issue cost (approximately $10,000 in legal fees). However, the breakthrough has been the acceptance of European documentation by US investors that are seeking higher yields and, at the same time, becoming more comfortable with the less-costly (that is, for the issuer) European documentation and disclosure practices. The issues that are easiest to place in this context are the more straightforward, plain vanilla deals.

The global private placement is particularly useful for borrowers because (1) the amounts they require are often too small for traditional Eurobond issues and (2) regulations that govern their financing activities can be rather complex, necessitating the exchange of special information which is easier in a private placement. These global placements fill a niche for relatively small, information-intensive deals.

Investors in different regions also look for different characteristics of the issue. Investors in the Netherlands prefer long-dated bonds issued by high-quality names. The more speculative, derivative-linked instruments are more often sold in Germany and southern Europe. The more popular derivative-linked private placements are duration-enhanced. In this arena, the distinction between a Euro medium-term note (EMTN) and a private placement is sometimes difficult to see.[11]

- If the investor is attempting to take a particular position with respect to interest rate exposure, the instrument is more likely an EMTN.
- On the other hand, if the borrower is attempting to satisfy a special financing need, the instrument is a private placement.

---

[11] See the section on *Medium-term notes*.

EMTN investors are very sensitive to price volatility, while private-placement investors are more concerned with the structure of the deal and yield during the holding period.

FACILITATING GROWTH OF THE FIRM

Whether it is raised through bank financing, long-term debt, or equity capital, whether it is publicly or privately issued, capital is the lifeblood of the business organization. With capital funds, the firm is able to invest in the assets that are required to generate revenues and profits.

WHY THE COST OF CAPITAL IS IMPORTANT AND HOW IT IS MANAGED

Introduction

■

Decisions that Affect the Suppliers of Capital

■

The Impact of Optimal Decisions

■

Bond Ratings and the Cost of Capital

■

Securitization and the Cost of Capital

■

Attention to the Cost of Capital

■

Securitization: Managing Credit Risk

INTRODUCTION

Chapter 1 described various sources of capital. Each of these sources of capital is associated with some cost. Bank debt and bonds carry either fixed or variable rates of interest. Stock is associated with the payment of dividends and, in most cases, investors' expectation of capital gains – increases in the market value of the stock.

Thus, the *cost of capital* is connected to the expectations of lenders and investors – the suppliers of capital. In turn, the expectations of suppliers of capital will drive the selection of long-term investment for the firm. That is, if investors require a relatively high rate of return, the firm will be obliged to consider only those projects that will satisfy the expectations. In general, higher risk is associated with higher rates of return. As a result, the cost of capital will affect the entire fabric of the company.

Various methods are used to interpret relative levels of risk, most notably bond ratings. Such ratings are closely guarded by companies because the ratings not only reflect the riskiness of the firm, but they also help define the universe of potential investors. Many institutional investors are prohibited from investing in companies with bond ratings below a certain level.

Financing structures have been devised to address the issue of the level of cost of capital. Securitization is one example. Through this process, risk associated with the issuer of securities is less important than the collateral backing the issue. Having been initiated in the financial institutions sector, securitization is increasingly used by nonfinancial corporations as a new method of raising capital while simultaneously lowering the cost of capital.

DECISIONS THAT AFFECT THE SUPPLIERS OF CAPITAL

Any decision concerning the asset base of the firm will have a direct impact on the financial claims of the suppliers of capital. Each decision affects the cash flows of the firm and, thus, the availability of interest and dividend payments. The full spectrum of corporation decisions will impact the cost of capital:

- new property, plant, and equipment
- new product lines
- acquisitions of other businesses.

New Property, Plant, and Equipment

The acquisition of fixed assets – property, plant, and equipment – has a profound effect on the cash flow stream of an organization. These assets establish the operating cash flows of the firm.

In the use of fixed assets, revenues are generated from the manufacture of goods or the provision of services. The utilization of (1) capital assets and (2) inputs of material and labor generate cash outflows. Net operating cash flow is the difference between the revenues and cash outflows (including any tax effects).

Net operating cash flows = Revenues – Operating outflows – Taxes

Net operating cash flows are then available to the suppliers of capital as interest payments, dividend payments, the repayment of debt capital, and the repurchase of equity, as applicable.[1] If net operating cash flows are fairly predictable, the level of risk perceived by suppliers of capital will be relatively low. Likewise, the minimum *required rate of return or cost of capital* will also be *relatively low*. On the other hand, if net operating cash flows have considerable volatility, the availability of funds to suppliers of capital will be less certain and the *required rate of return* will be *relatively high*.

---

[1] Technically, interest payments on debt are deductible for tax purposes while dividend payments, debt principal repayments, and stock repurchases are not. This means that there is a tax benefit associated with the use of debt financing. See Chapter 3 for a discussion of this effect.

When new fixed assets are acquired, the risk associated with acquisitions is directly related to the cost of capital. If the new assets are expected to have the same level of cash flow volatility, the cost of capital will change very little, if at all. If the new assets are expected to have significant cash flow implications, the cost of capital will also change.

- Less volatile incremental cash flows will lower the cost of capital.
- More volatile incremental cash flows will raise the cost of capital.

For example, consider a new capital asset that reduces the amount of required troubleshooting in the production process. Assume that the greatest number of production problems occurs when the firm is changing production setups. If the new asset can reduce the labor and materials associated with production transitions, net operating cash flows will be less volatile. The cost of capital will be lower.

Consider another example. A new piece of capital equipment has a much more involved maintenance program and will create higher costs of operation. The attraction of the new equipment may be that it enables the firm to shift quickly among the several production setups, significantly reducing lead time. In turn, the reduction in lead time makes the firm more competitive and able to win production contracts that it previously could not win. When the firm is realizing the revenues associated with new contracts, revenues are higher than normal. However, during the times when there are no new contracts, net cash flows are lower because of the maintenance requirements. Thus, this equipment creates more volatility which will be reflected in the cost of capital.

New Product Lines

When a company introduces a new product line, the suppliers of capital, again, will be affected. New products can either (1) add to the overall stream of cash flows in a fairly consistent way, (2) add to the overall cash flow stream in a less predictable fashion, or (3) add cash flows and, at the same time, reduce cash flows from existing product lines.

In the first case, a new product line that extends the current technology and is a natural complement to the existing product line may likely add little volatility to the cash flow stream. Accordingly, the cost of capital will not change significantly.

On the other hand, a new product that takes the company into relatively uncharted territory may require some length of time to become accepted in the market. During this time, revenues may be modest, albeit increasing. In the meantime, cash outflows for production and product marketing may generate losses – introducing volatility in the cash flow stream. The volatility will increase the cost of capital because there is now more operational risk involved.

The most risky new product introduction is one that will compete with the existing products. In this case, cash flow volatility has two sources:

- volatility associated with a new product offering;
- volatility associated with potential market erosion (cannibalization) of existing products' market share.

All other things equal, the cost of capital will be highest in this scenario.

Acquiring Other Businesses

The acquisition of other businesses is similar to the addition of new products and can be analyzed in a similar way. However, on the spectrum of volatility and risk, this activity has the highest probability of introducing greater risk into operational cash flows and, thus, increasing the cost of capital.

If the new business is in the same industry, the probability of increased risk is diminished. In fact, there may be aspects of cost reduction when redundancies are eliminated – for example, in administrative functions. In fact, such efficiencies have contributed to the current consolidation of the banking and insurance industries. However, if the businesses are dissimilar, a number of factors will increase volatility of operational cash flows. The issues may be classified as follows:

- communicating operational information among the affected groups of workers and managers;
- communicating the advantages of such a combination to the customers/clients of the firm;
- establishing and implementing common product quality standards;
- integrating communications systems;
- establishing satisfactory terms of trade with suppliers and vendors of the acquired company;
- effectively communicating the satisfactory resolution of all of the above to the investing public – including institutional investors.

All of the uncertainties associated with these issues will increase the cost of capital because the suppliers of capital potentially will be at greater risk.

Nevertheless, acquiring other businesses can lead to significant diversification of operational cash flows – a benefit to suppliers of capital. Diversification reduces exposure to one industry, which may be subject to normal business-cycle volatility. If this is the case, the cost of capital will decline.

Portfolio Implications for the Cost of Capital

Whenever a firm purchases new equipment, enters a new product line, or acquires another business, the suppliers of capital will be impacted and the cost of capital may change. Whether there is a change in the cost of capital when one of these events occurs depends on two factors:

- level and volatility of cash flows associated with the new activity;
- correlation of cash flows between the new activity and the existing activities.

Chapters 3 and 4 develop the concept of cost of capital as it relates to the first factor. The second factor suggests that there are portfolio implications whenever the firm introduces a new activity. Chapter 5 discusses the application of portfolio theory to the cost of capital.

THE IMPACT OF OPTIMAL DECISIONS

Ultimately, the decisions discussed in the previous section will affect the cost of capital and the *value of the firm* and, accordingly, the *stock price*. Management objective should be to maximize both.

The Value of the Firm

The value of the firm is directly related to:

- operating cash flows of the firm
- cost of capital.

The value of these cash flows is equivalent to the value of the firm from the perspective of all of the suppliers of capital.

First, in a no-growth scenario, the cash flows do not change and their value is that of a perpetuity.[2]

$$V_F = \frac{CF}{k}$$

where V_F = value of a perpetuity

CF = periodic cash flow

k = discount rate

Specifically, in valuing assumed perpetual cash flows of a firm, the value is determined by using the *weighted average cost of capital* (WACC).

$$V_F = \frac{CF}{WACC}$$

where V_F = value of a firm

CF = periodic cash flow

WACC = weighted average cost of capital

= combined cost of all suppliers of capital

---

[2] A perpetuity is a stream of equal cash flows that does not end.

Thus, in a mature company, in which operational cash flows can be assumed to be level, the value of the firm will depend on the combined cost of capital of all suppliers of capital. All other things equal, the lower the WACC, the higher the value of the firm. Clearly, financial managers have a vested interest in achieving a low cost of capital.

When growth of cash flows is assumed, the model for firm valuation is adjusted for g, the long-run, sustainable growth rate.

$$V_F = \frac{CF_1}{WACC - g}$$

where CF_1 = next period's cash flow

= current CF increased at a constant rate of growth

= $CF_0(1 + g)$

g = long-run, sustainable growth rate

The introduction of a growth factor increases the value of the firm.[3] Again, the lower the cost of capital, the higher the value of the firm.

The Stock Price

A link exists between cost of capital and the price of a firm's stock. Shareholders receive dividend payments and they also realize capital gains or losses.[4] The rates of return to shareholders are based on these cash flows.

- The **capital gains yield** is roughly equivalent to g, the firm's long-run sustainable growth rate.
- The **dividend yield** is a more short-term measure – the projected annual dividend as a percentage of the current stock price.

$$\text{Dividend yield} = \frac{D_1}{P_0}$$

---

[3] Mathematically, subtracting g reduces the denominator which increases the value of the ratio.
[4] Capital gains and losses are increases and decreases in the market value of an asset.

To illustrate the connection between stock price and cost of capital, assume a no-growth situation. When there is no growth in the stock price, the dividend yield becomes effectively the total return to the shareholder. That is, when $g = 0$, there is no capital gains yield and the dividend yield is the only remaining return to shareholders.

The no-growth scenario is based on an assumption that all earnings will be paid to shareholders as dividends. In other words, there will be no growth if no future earnings are reinvested in the firm. Since all earnings are paid as dividends, earnings equal dividends and dividend per share equals earnings per share. It also follows that the dividend yield can be expressed as a ratio: *dividend per share/price* or *earnings per share/price*.

$$D_1 = E_1$$

$$\frac{D_1}{P_0} = \frac{E_1}{P_0}$$

However, notice that $\frac{E_1}{P_0}$ is the inverse of the $\frac{P}{E}$ ratio. Thus, in a no-growth situation, the inverse of the $\frac{P}{E}$ ratio is the required return to a shareholder.

Suppose that a company's stock was selling at a $\frac{P}{E}$ ratio of 7. This can be interpreted as a minimum required rate of return to shareholders of 14.3 percent.

$$\frac{1}{\left(\frac{P}{E}\right)} = \text{required return for shareholders}$$

$$= \frac{1}{7}$$

$$\cong 0.143$$

$$\cong 14.3\%$$

In this case, 14.3 percent rate of return must be incorporated into the cost of capital used to fund projects. If new equipment, product lines, or businesses do not return at least 14.3 percent to equity holders, the market will force down the price of the stock.

Thus, there is a close link between changes in the stock price and changes in the cost of capital. The appropriate assessment of the cost of capital of the firm is critical in the financial management function. Furthermore, efforts to minimize the cost of capital will help optimize the price of the stock for all shareholders.

2

BOND RATINGS AND THE COST OF CAPITAL

The cost of capital is directly related to perceived risk of the issuer of a security. Risk of a debt issue is frequently estimated by rating agencies. Two debt leading rating agencies in the USA with global activities are Standard & Poor's Corporation (S&P) and Moody's Investors Service.[5] S&P bond ratings range from AAA to D (see Figure 2.1).

Standard & Poor's also assigns + or – to ratings in order to further differentiate bond quality.

---

[5] Other rating services include Fitch Investor's Service and Duff & Phelps.

FIGURE 2.1
S&P Bond Ratings
AAA: Highest rating, suggesting the obligor has extremely strong ability to pay principal and interest.
AA: High-quality issuance with very strong repayment capacity, differing from AAA only by a small degree. Ability of obligor to meet financial commitment is very strong.
A: Upper medium grade with strong capacity to pay principal and interest but somewhat more susceptible to adverse economic conditions. Ability of obligor to meet financial commitment is strong.
BBB: Medium grade with adequate capacity to pay principal and interest. It is more likely that adverse economic conditions or changing conditions will lead to a weakened capacity of obligor to meet its financial commitment.
BB, B, CCC, CC, C: Ability to pay principal and interest is to a greater or lesser degree speculative: BB – predominantly speculative. Adverse conditions could lead to the obligor's inability to meet the financial obligation.   B – speculative, low grade. Adverse conditions would likely impair obligor's inability to meet the financial obligation.   CCC – poor quality. Adverse conditions will likely lead to obligor's inability to meet financial obligation.   CC – high speculation. Obligation is highly vulnerable to nonpayment.   C – highest speculation. Bankruptcy petition may have been filed or a similar action may have been taken, but payments on the obligation are continuing.
CI: Rated debt instrument is an income bond on which interest is not being paid, lowest quality.[6]
DDD, DD, D: Bond is in default and principal and/or interest are in arrears: DDD – in default (issuer's failure to meet one or more of the contractual obligations of the bond indenture).   DD – in arrears (bond interest due but unpaid, after any allowed grace period).   D – questionable value.

---

[6] An income bond pays interest only if the issuing firm earns enough income.

Moody's ratings are similar. Figure 2.2 shows the S&P's ratings with the equivalent Moody's ratings.

FIGURE 2.2	
Comparison of S&P's Ratings and Moody's Ratings	
S&P's rating	**Moody's rating**
AAA	Aaa
AA+ AA AA–	Aa1 Aa2 Aa3
A+ A A–	A1 A2 A3
BBB+ BBB BBB–	Baa1 Baa2 Baa3
BB+ BB BB–	Ba1 Ba2 Ba3
B+ B B–	B1 B2 B3
CCC+ CCC CCC–	Caa
CC	Ca
C	C

2
___

Ratings are based on a number of *quantitative* and *qualitative* criteria. Basic quantitative considerations include the firm's debt and its debt servicing capacity. Structural aspects of bond issues are also evaluated – mortgage, subordination, guarantee provisions, sinking fund, and maturity – as applicable. Quantitative factors that are relevant to the firm's particular operating environment may include sales stability and unfunded pension liabilities. Qualitative factors that are important to the operating environment include labor relations, resource availability, government regulatory issues, environmental issues, and political risk exposure in overseas operations.

Bonds rated AAA through BBB are considered *investment grade* securities. Many financial institutions are not allowed to invest in securities other than investment grade – commercial banks, fiduciaries (who administer investments for others), mutual savings banks, and trust companies (corporations that accept and execute trust funds). From an issuer's perspective, the higher bond ratings mean that investors will require lower rates of return. Understandably, firms are careful to protect their bond ratings. There is a direct relationship between bond ratings and the cost of capital.

SECURITIZATION AND THE COST OF CAPITAL

Securitization is the process of converting loans and other financial assets into securities that are sold to investors, thus creating asset-backed securities. Securitization provides a significant advantage to corporations. Fully collateralized financing means that the issuer can obtain funds at a lower cost of capital.

Assets That May Be Securitized

US government agencies had a major role in the development of the asset-backed securities market, having introduced the first pass-through securities during the 1970s with *mortgage loans* as collateral. These initial issuances have been followed by private-sector issues and innovation in terms of underlying assets which now include *automobile loans*, *credit card receivables*, *commercial loans*, *computer and truck leases*, *loans for mobile homes*, and *other trade receivables*.

In addition to asset-backed bonds, commercial paper and preferred stock has been issued with asset backing. Usually, commercial paper is secured by credit card receivables, automobile and utility leases, and trade receivables. Preferred stock is frequently secured by mortgage-backed securities and trade receivables.

Both asset-backed commercial paper and preferred stock have interest or dividend payments that are *not* tied to the cash flows of the *underlying* assets. In the case of asset-backed preferred stock, the dividend rate is auction-rated. The dividends on this stock are paid and adjusted quarterly – based on a spread over government securities rates. Because of this frequent change in the dividend rate, the market price of this preferred stock remains very close to par value. These adjustable-rate issues have no maturity date, but may often be called at the option of the issuer.

With respect to asset-backed commercial paper, these programs typically do not "unwind" when underlying assets amortize. That is, the commercial paper is not paid off when the original collateral assets are paid off. Instead, new receivables are bought continually, with the net effect that the commercial paper is rolled over when it matures.

Choosing a Form of Securitization

Various forms of securitization are possible. Generally, there are three basic categories:

- pass-through securities
- asset-backed bonds
- pay-through bonds.

Pass-through Securities

Pass-through securities pay investors their proportional shares of cash flows generated by underlying assets. These cash flows include both principal and interest payments. A fee for servicing the underlying assets is deducted from each interest payment. A pass-through security, thus, represents ownership in a pool of assets. The assets are removed from the balance sheet of the originator of the loans and placed in a *trust*. In turn, the trust issues certificates of ownership to investors, the effective owners of the underlying assets.

Because the assets in the pool are typically mortgage loans and consumer receivables (automobile loans and credit card receivables), payments on the loans are generated monthly. All cash flows, with the exception of the servicing fee, flow to investors. These payments include interest, principal, and any prepayments of principal. Thus, cash flows from the underlying assets are said to be *dedicated* cash flows.

Asset-backed Bonds

Asset-backed bonds remain on the balance sheet of the issuer. Underlying assets collateralize the bonds and also remain on the balance sheet of the issuer. The underlying assets may be loans or pass-through securities. As is true with other types of bonds, interest is paid semiannually and the face amount (par value or maturity value) is paid upon maturity. One characteristic of asset-backed bonds is that they are typically overcollateralized, that is, the value of underlying assets is greater than the face value of asset-backed bonds. Each quarter, the value of the underlying assets (collateral) is assessed. If this amount is less than the amount specified in the bond indenture, additional loans or pass-through securities must be added to the collateral.

Unlike pass-through securities, asset-backed bonds do not have dedicated cash flows from the underlying assets. Also, because assets remain on the balance sheet of the issuer, no trust is formed.

Pay-through Bonds

Pay-through bonds are a hybrid of pass-through securities and asset-backed bonds. Pay-through bonds are obligations of the issuer, as are asset-backed bonds. However, all cash flows are dedicated to servicing the obligation represented by pay-through bonds and a separate entity is formed to hold the underlying assets, as is the case with pass-through securities. This separate entity also issues the bonds. Interest and principal payments are made monthly or quarterly.

Unlike either pass-through securities or asset-backed bonds, pay-through bonds are issued in different *tranches*.[7] An *accrual* or *accretion bond* is similar to a zero-coupon bond, and is frequently referred to as a *Z-bond*. This Z-bond tranche receives no interest or principal until it matures. Other tranches receive payments of interest at regular intervals. Commonly, only one tranche receives principal payments at a time. When principal has been repaid for the first tranche, then the second tranche begins to receive principal payments. When the second tranche has been completely repaid with respect to principal, the third tranche begins to receive principal payments.

The pay-through bond structure is intended to eliminate much of the uncertainty with respect to *prepayment risk*. Prepayment risk is the exposure that a long-term investor faces when purchasing an amortizing security that is repaid much earlier than the original maturity date. While the investor may realize a gain on the early return of principal, the anticipated stream of interest payments can be drastically reduced. Pay-through bonds give investors relatively more control over this eventuality.

Pay-through bonds may also contain a residual tranche which receives cash flows that are in excess of the obligations to the other tranches. This may occur, for example, when the rate of prepayment that is anticipated at the time of securitization exceeds the actual rate of prepayment, that is, the underlying assets are not amortized as quickly as originally antici-pated. When this occurs, total interest payments are greater than other-wise would have been the case. These "excess" interest payments accrue to the residual tranche investor.

Each tranche is intended to satisfy a different investor preference for cash flows in terms of interest, principal, and timing of each. Along with the collateral (underlying assets), the structure of pay-through bonds – geared to accommodate liquidity preferences of investors – helps to reduce the cost of debt capital. Figure 2.3 summarizes the basic charac-

---

[7] A tranche is a portion of a securities issue. Literally, the word means "slice."

FIGURE 2.3			
Types of Asset-Backed Securities			
	Pass-through securities	**Asset-backed bonds**	**Pay-through bonds**
Payment frequency	Monthly	Semiannually	Monthly or quarterly
Recorded on the balance sheet of the issuer?	No	Yes	No
Cash flows from underlying assets dedicated to investors?	Yes	No	Yes
Trust or other separate entity created?	Yes	No	Yes
Classes of securities	Same for all investors	Same for all investors	Different tranches within one issue

teristics of pass-throughs, asset-backed bonds, and pay-through bonds. The pass-through securities are the first generation of asset-backed securities, while pay-through bonds are the most recent development in the market. In each case, however, the credit rating of the underlying assets – rather than the credit rating of the issuing firm – determines the cost of capital associated with the issue.

The Securitization Process

While each securitization has its own unique structure, certain aspects are almost universal:

- originators
- servicers
- investment bankers
- credit enhancers
- trustees
- credit rating agencies.

Originators

Originators make the loans or create the assets that become the collateral for asset-backed securities. The entities involved in originating these assets are varied: federal agencies, commercial banks, savings and loan associations, captive finance companies (especially those affiliated with automobile manufacturers), other finance companies, computer companies, manufacturing firms, life insurance companies, and securities firms. Among the assets that are securitized by these originators are: residential mortgage loans, automobile loans, mobile home loans, computer leases, trade receivables, and policyholder loans. Recently, intellectual property assets have been securitized:

- Walt Disney film receipts ($400 million, 1992)
- Calvin Klein perfume product sales ($58 million, 1993)
- GE Capital trademarks (1995, amount not available)
- Nestlé trademarks and brand assets (1996, amount not available)
- Universal Studios film receivables ($1.1 billion, 1997)
- Rod Stewart music royalties ($15.4 million, 1998)
- PolyGram film receipts ($650 million, 1998)
- Cecchi Gori 1,200-film portfolio (Italian media group, 500 billion lira, 1998)
- New Line Cinema film portfolio ($350 million, 1998)
- Holland-Dozier-Holland music royalties ($30 million, 1998).

Thus, the range of assets that can be considered for securitization continues to widen, as does the circle of originators.

Servicers

Servicers manage the underlying assets in the securitization process – collecting principal and interest payments, maintaining records, and performing necessary collection functions. Servicers also generate monthly or annual reports with respect to the underlying assets and the value of the portfolio. In most cases, the originators or affiliates of the originators act as servicers.

Issuers

The entities that actually offer the asset-backed securities are *issuers*. Typically, originators do not sell the asset-backed securities directly to investors. A "bankruptcy-remote" finance company is usually created. Alternative names for the issuing finance company are:

■ conduit
■ special purpose vehicle (SPV)
■ special purpose entity (SPE)
■ limited purpose corporation.

Issuers may either be subsidiaries of the originators or subsidiaries of the investment bankers. When the issuer is a subsidiary of the investment banker, it is often referred to as an *orphan subsidiary*. Issuers become bankruptcy-remote by issuing no other debt besides the asset-backed securities. In the event that additional debt is issued by the issuer, it is subordinated to the asset-backed securities and the priority of the claims of holders of the asset-backed securities is in no way diminished by the additional debt. In this way, the risk assumed by investors in the asset-backed securities is not increased.

In some cases, the asset-backed securities of one issuer are collateralized by assets that have been created by several originators. This situation is beneficial in those cases in which individual originators have insufficient assets to create a pool that is large enough for securitization. Thus, medium-sized companies can realize cost efficiencies associated with securitization.

Investment Bankers

Investment bankers place the asset-backed securities with investors. If the issue is a public placement, the underwriter purchases these securities and then resells them to the public. If the issue is a private placement, the investment banker acts as agent to assemble an adequate group of investors. A private placement involves less risk for the underwriter and, accordingly, a lower underwriting fee. However, a private placement is also less liquid than a public placement. As a result, the interest rate associated with privately placed asset-backed securities will be higher than with a public issue. In either case, the investment banker, together with the issuer, structures the issue and ensures compliance with all legal, accounting, and regulatory requirements. The commitment of time and resources by an investment banker will be greater, all other things being equal, for a first-time issue, an issue by an infrequent issuer, or a new type of issue.

Credit Enhancers

Credit enhancers improve the credit rating and, thus, the marketability of an issue. Most asset-backed securities are credit enhanced either by the issuer or by a third party. Third party-credit enhancement takes the form of a *letter of credit* or *private insurance*. On the other hand, the issuer can enhance an issue by establishing a senior-subordinated structure, over-collateralization, or establishing a spread account.

- In a senior-subordinated structure, the originator assumes risk by holding the subordinated securities.
- Overcollateralization is used primarily in those structures that have been referred to above as asset-backed bonds, that is, bonds that remain on the balance sheet of the originator. The objective of overcollateralization is to protect the investor from deterioration in the market value of the collateral.
- A spread account is established by the servicer. Upon issue, a spread account receives an advance from the servicer. After issue, any excess of cash flows beyond those necessary to make promised payments to

investors and to cover servicing fees accrues to the spread account. At the time of maturity, any remaining balance in the spread account is returned to the servicer.

Trustees

Trustees, together with issuers, establish the trusts that are part of the structure of asset-backed securities. A trust is composed of the underlying assets and (1) has the right to receive payments due on the underlying assets, (2) has security interests in the collateral for the underlying assets (for example residences that collateralize underlying mortgages), and (3) may be beneficiaries of any insurance, including credit enhancement. A trustee is the liaison between the servicer of the asset-backed security and the investors. A trustee also acts as the contact between a credit enhancer and the investors. Standard & Poor's, the debt rating agency, sets the minimum acceptable capital level of a trustee for an asset-backed issue at $500 million. In practice, the trustees for virtually every issue of asset-backed securities that are not mortgage-related have been large money center commercial banks. The responsibilities of the trustee may be summarized as follows:

- purchasing assets from the issuer on behalf of the trust;
- issuing certificates to investors;
- when the servicer deposits funds in the trust account, passing these on to investors;
- reinvesting funds in the trust account if there is a time lag between date of deposit and date of payment to investors;
- determining that reports made by the servicer to investors are adequate;
- distributing servicer reports to investors;
- performing the functions of the servicer if the servicer is unable to do so.

Notice that the trustee helps to maintain the distance between the originator and the investor. This arrangement works to support the independent credit evaluation of the securitized assets, helping to lower the cost of capital.

Credit Rating Agencies

Credit rating agencies perform the same function for asset-backed securities as they do for conventional bonds. In this evaluation, credit rating agencies consider the creditworthiness of the issuer (a special purpose finance company subsidiary of either the originator or the underwriting investment banker). However, the creditworthiness of the conduit is related to the underlying assets. A rating agency must evaluate how likely it is that the issuer will be able to deliver all promised payments of principal and interest. The ability to deliver promised payments, in turn, is related to the structure of the issue – underlying assets, the servicer, the trustee, and the credit enhancer.

2

How Feasible Is Securitization?

Several questions can help financial managers decide whether securitization might be a feasible alternative.

- Are the credit issues relatively easy to understand and communicate?
- How easily can the cash flows of the underlying assets be estimated?
- Will the average life of the underlying assets be at least one year, ensuring an adequate return of interest payments?
- What are the historical default rates of the underlying assets?
- Do the underlying assets totally amortize?
- Are the underlying assets based on a diverse pool?
- Can the collateral of the underlying assets (for example, the homes that are collateral for mortgages) be easily liquidated, as necessary?

To the extent that the answers to these questions are favorable, the securitization will be less costly. All these factors contribute to the liquidity of the issue, the size of the potential investor pool, and the reduction of the cost of capital.

ATTENTION TO THE COST OF CAPITAL

The cost of capital must be considered whenever a firm purchases new fixed assets, develops new product lines, or acquires other businesses. The appropriate assessment of the required return for providers of capital is essential in order to optimize the value of the firm and to maximize shareholder wealth. The lower the cost of capital, the higher the value of the firm.

Market analysts continually evaluate a firm's riskiness and an important part of this risk assessment is the cost of debt. Bond ratings are closely guarded since lower perceived risk results in higher ratings and lower required rates of return by investors. Various mechanisms have been developed to effect lower risk perceptions. Notably, securitization has become an increasingly significant method of lowering risk by capitalizing on the strength of the balance sheet to secure borrowings at the lowest possible cost.

SECURITIZATION: MANAGING CREDIT RISK

The complexity of an asset-backed security suggests that its components must be analyzed individually. There are three main questions that should be answered:

- What is the credit quality of the underlying assets and the entities involved in the transaction, including the originator, the servicer, the issuer, the trustee, and the credit enhancers?
- Will the cash flows from the underlying assets (including credit enhancements and liquidity supports) be sufficient to meet payment obligations to investors with respect to interest and principal?
- Is the issuer (conduit) structured in such a way that holders of the asset-backed securities have legally binding rights to the cash flows generated by the underlying assets in the event of financial distress?

Because there are separate responsibilities at every level of the securitization, the functions have become quite fragmented. It is necessary to evaluate each function clearly and distinctly even when two or more functions are performed by the same party. In every case, the responsibilities and contingencies associated with each function must be clearly outlined in the documentation for the transaction.

The Asset Pool

2

Portfolio performance of the asset pool is perhaps the most critical element of evaluating the creditworthiness of an asset-backed security. Pertinent issues include projected portfolio delinquency, default rates, and the severity of loss in periods of economic distress. Asset pools can generally be classified in one of three categories – consumer assets, commercial assets, and focus (other assets).

Consumer assets (secured and unsecured) include retail auto loans, auto leases, credit card receivables, residential mortgage loans, and home equity loans (second mortgages). Pools of these assets, and assets like these, are typically large (250 to 500 individual loans), creating diversification benefits in the asset pool itself. In addition, such loans are often originated with homogeneous credit standards and terms.

Because of these characteristics, consumer assets may be analyzed with historical statistics that provide much information about the future cash flows associated with the underlying assets. However, it should be noted that studies which formally correlate underwriting criteria to portfolio performance have been rare outside the residential mortgage market. Nevertheless, specific factors such as loan-to-value ratios, property types, amortization schedules, and other factors are important variables in the evaluation of an asset pool of consumer loans.

Commercial assets include equipment loans and leases, dealer inventory financing (floor plans), and trade receivables. In these cases, each loan will typically be larger in amount. As a result, the pool may only include 50 individual credits (as compared to as many as 500 in a consumer asset pool). In these cases, the larger transactions will probably be reviewed individually while smaller transactions are sampled. The results of the credit review will then be weighted by the relative importance within the asset pool to assess overall creditworthiness.

Focus assets are even less standardized. These assets require a special "focus" on the legal and cash flow patterns not found in other assets. Examples of these are franchise agreements, special licensing, oil and gas rights, and mortgage servicing rights. In these cases, specialized credit evaluation criteria must be developed that depend on the underlying assets.

Ideally, *information* about the asset pool will include:

- aggregate pool balance as of the cut-off date
- number of loans or leases
- average loan or lease balance
- weighted average yield
- range of interest rates
- weighted average remaining time to maturity
- the range of remaining time to maturity
- weighted average original time to maturity
- range of original time to maturity
- weighted average loan-to-value ratio (secured assets)
- range of loan-to-value ratios
- new/used ratios (automobiles, boats, mobile homes, and equipment)
- geographic distribution (state, city)
- prepayment provisions and penalties
- cash flow projections
- fees (for example, late fees)
- historical payments, including interest and principal
- historical purchase rate (especially for credit cards – rate at which balance of the underlying loans will increase after securitization)
- average credit limits
- delinquency status of loans

■ concentration of obligors (individuals, industries, or other common characteristics).

This is not a complete list of pool characteristics, but it does serve to illustrate the need for all relevant information about cash flows of the asset pool. So that risk may be assessed adequately, a minimum of three years of data is required. Preferably, a five-year stream of information should be provided. Delinquency status and past performance of the pool have the highest correlations with asset pool performance. Thus, historical data is extremely important.

Once the pool has been analyzed, it may be necessary to *adjust the pool* to make it more attractive to investors. This internal enhancement of the pool may take one of two forms:

■ restructuring the pool
■ setting termination triggers.

Restructuring the pool means eliminating those individual assets that cause the asset pool to contain either undesirable receivables, excessive concentrations, or a higher-than-desired loss probability. One possible method of eliminating undesirable receivables is to remove any loans or other receivables that are overdue at the time of pool assessment. Under other circumstances, it may be desirable to eliminate assets with an original term to maturity over a specified maximum.

Such selection filters will depend on the nature of the asset pool and the perceived preferences of investors. Eliminating excessive concentrations may reduce exposure to specific industries, geographic regions, or other variables that would suggest an unacceptable reduction of diversification. Examples might include eliminating any assets that represent more than a 10 percent concentration within a particular industry. Again, the specific filter will depend on the portfolio and perceived investor preferences.

The objective of restructuring the pool is to reduce maximum anticipated loss to an acceptable level. In order to achieve this, it is necessary to associate a probability of loss with each individual asset in the pool. By multiplying this probability (or anticipated loss proportion) by the face amount of the asset, a dollar amount of anticipated loss can be generated. When the results of this calculation are summed across all assets in the asset pool, the expected loss of the entire portfolio may be estimated.

$$EL = \sum_{i=1}^{N} p_i A_i$$

where EL = expected loss

p_i = loss proportion of asset i

A_i = face amount of asset i

N = total number of individual assets

Clearly, calculating expected loss is not a precise science because it requires a subjective assessment of future loss. However, the evaluation serves an important function in that it focuses on expectations in connection with each of the assets of the pool. This permits subsequent monitoring of the asset pool to be framed in the context of variance from expectations.

If the asset pool consists of receivables that require regular asset substitutions, the integrity of the entire pool can be protected by instituting *termination triggers*. The substitution may be necessary when short-term assets are used as collateral for the asset-backed security. Examples of such short-term arrangements include credit card receivables or trade receivables. A termination trigger prevents deterioration in the asset portfolio of the originator from contaminating the asset pool of the asset-backed security. Suppose, for example, that the historical default rate on the originator's loan portfolio is 1 percent per year. The termination trigger may require that no further assets be transferred into the trust if the originator's default experience increases to 2 percent per year. In this case, the asset-backed security would accept no further assets from the originator.

Should the same factors that impacted the originator's loan portfolio begin to impact assets held in trust for the asset-backed security, pre-arranged credit enhancements would protect investors. That is, excessive default losses would be absorbed by the credit enhancer, rather than the investors in the asset-backed security.

The Originator

The credit risk associated with the *originator* falls into several categories:

- legal risk associated with asset transfers;
- the potential effect of the originator's bankruptcy on the quality of the assets in the pool;
- the necessary credit support to protect investors.

The originator generally *transfers assets* to the asset pool through a *true sale* or a *transfer of title*. The process involves amending certificates of title.[8] If title is not amended, investors may not be permitted to benefit from the sale of the collateral for the underlying loans and receivables in the event of bankruptcy. That is, the sale of collateral may accrue to creditors of the originator instead of to investors in the asset-backed security. Also, in the event of bankruptcy, a credit card asset pool may be prohibited from receiving additional individual assets as stipulated in the indenture for the asset-backed security. It should be noted that this is less of a problem with financial institutions than with retail operations. For example, if a savings and loan association becomes insolvent, the credit card portfolio may be absorbed by a stronger financial institution that takes over the failed thrift. On the other hand, a retail operation may be unwound with no new receivables generated.

An *originator's bankruptcy* can also impact an asset-backed security in ways that are not directly related to credit. When individual assets are collateralized by vehicles or other equipment, the quality of service for the collateral will deteriorate if the originator – the manufacturer – becomes

---

[8] In the USA, the transfer of assets may involve filing a UCC-1 financing statement. UCC is an acronym for the Uniform Commercial Code, a set of standardized state laws that govern financial contracts. Contracts covered by the UCC include negotiable instruments (checks, drafts, and other negotiable instruments), bank deposits, letters of credit, warehouse receipts, other documents of title, and secured loans.

insolvent. If the manufacturer of the collateral has financial difficulties, this may impact the quality of the collateral itself, prompting transaction disputes and product returns. In turn, nonpayment on individual pool assets will result. Such nonpayment circumstances are referred to as *dilution* of trade receivables or retail credit card receivables.

Both these concerns (effective ownership of pool assets and potential for dilution) will have an impact on the appropriate level of *credit enhancement*. Specific provisions for credit enhancement may be necessary to compensate for potential disputes over title of individual assets in the asset pool and dilution of the receivables.

As a result of these considerations, the credit of the originator is a crucial element in evaluating a potential asset-backed security. The areas that should be examined are:

- sourcing of credit or loan applications submitted to the originator
- credit review of applications
- appraisals of collateral (as applicable)
- credit approval guidelines
- documentation of loans
- loan disbursement procedures
- overall loan portfolio performance
- representations and warranties of the originator as compared to actual portfolio performance.

Figure 2.4 contains the credit ratings that may be given to an originator by Standard & Poor's. These ratings range from "Strong" to "Weak." A rating of "Strong" can be earned by an originator that has a management team that is competent in the area of underwriting practices. The rating agency also expects that conservative standards have been set in terms of generating individual assets. There is an implicit expectation that the originator has made an adequate investment in technology so that in-house information management is more than adequate for the assets in the pool and for ongoing operations. Ability to service assets is important because many originators are also servicers.

FIGURE 2.4	
Credit Rating of the Originator of an Asset-backed Security	
S&P rating	**Characteristics of originator**
Strong	*Highest ranking:* Strong and stable management, highly effective production capacity, use of conservative underwriting standards to generate individual loans or receivables, quality control systems that exceed industry standards, superior loan servicing operations
Above average	*Differs from highest ranking only by a small margin:* Differences relate to track record, stability, flexibility, or financial condition
Average	*Variable track record:* Variability may relate to nontraditional underwriting standards to generate individual loans or receivables, delinquencies near the national average, loan servicing adequate but not incorporating the most recent industry innovations, overall improving performance
Below average	*Lack of ability, productivity, and competence:* Variable track record, underwriting consistently more liberal than traditional standards, marginal loan servicing capability, overall declining performance
Weak	*Poor track record:* Underwriting exclusively more liberal than traditional standards, inadequate quality control, recurring losses, servicing capability overextended, delinquencies far exceed national averages

Source: Griep, C. M. "Structured Securities: Credit, Cash Flow, and Legal Risks," *The Global Asset Backed Securities Market: Structuring, Managing and Allocating Risk*, by Store, C., Zissu, A., and Lederman, J. (eds), 1993, Probus, Chicago, pp. 140–1.

At the other extreme, a "Weak" rating is given to firms that have used underwriting standards that are much more liberal than the industry standards. A firm also might receive this rating when quality control is poor and the technology and human capital necessary to adequately service loans is inadequate. A firm with a "Weak" rating will also have experienced losses in its underwriting activities, often associated with high levels of delinquencies.

All of the above considerations are not to suggest that only the creditworthiness of the originator determines the viability of the securitized issue. However, serious problems with respect to the originator can doom a securitization to failure.

The Servicer

Most asset-backed securities transactions have direct credit exposure in connection with the *servicer*. The exposure arises because the servicer holds funds that will be distributed to investors. To the extent that servicers pass along payments from pool assets to the trustee on a daily basis, the exposure is minimized. However, some asset-backed securities are structured so that payments from the servicer to investors are at less frequent intervals than payments from pool assets to the servicer. For example, in some credit card asset-backed securities, the servicer may commingle funds for up to 70 days. In such a case, the exposure to servicer credit risk is relatively high.

According to the terms of the indenture, a servicer may also provide a cash advance to cover delinquencies that may be ultimately recoverable. This cash advance protects investors from uneven cash flows, that is, liquidity risk. The credit of the servicer is, in this case, directly linked to the creditworthiness of the asset-backed security. In evaluating the servicer, a number of variables are considered. In some cases these variables are similar to those that are scrutinized in an examination of the originator. Recall that the originator may, in some cases, continue to act as the servicer in a particular transaction. Nevertheless, the two functions are distinct and must be evaluated as such.

In the area of collections, a servicer must demonstrate the ability to meet servicing needs by having adequate staff and systems. The functions of the servicer that will be important are timing and prioritization of collection actions, policies and practices that involve rewriting or restructuring individual assets, terms relating to the extension of due dates, and forbearance policies (under some circumstances, declining to exercise a legal right against a borrower in default). Another important element of the responsibilities of a servicer are recovery procedures. Collecting amounts associated with previously defaulted individual assets will benefit investors either directly or indirectly in that these cash proceeds will help reimburse the expenses of collection activities.

Depending on the nature of the assets in the pool, servicers may have considerable discretion in managing the assets. For example, transactions that involve multifamily and commercial mortgages typically give servicers considerable discretion in loan restructuring, foreclosures, and other collection-related activities. A transaction should be structured to periodically review practices and procedures adopted and followed by the servicer.

The servicer should be evaluated along several basic criteria:

- servicing history
- servicing experience
- servicing capabilities
- origination policies and procedures (as applicable)
- management competence
- adequacy of staff
- potential for growth in the servicing industry
- degree of competition from other servicers
- overall business environment
- financial condition of servicer.

The financial condition of servicers can vary significantly. Some servicers are subsidiaries of originating entities, with adequate capital and capital reserves (in the form of parent company capitalization). In other cases, servicers are stand-alone operations with limited working capital. In the latter case, a servicer will be less able to add staff for either processing or collections when circumstances warrant. In all cases, a servicer should be able to demonstrate the ability to fulfill necessary functions throughout the life of the asset-backed security.

If there is a possibility that a servicer may not be able to fulfill its responsibilities under the terms of the transactions, provisions should be made for the substitution of servicers. Alternatively, a larger, better capitalized organization can be specified as a master servicer to which the responsibility would fall in the event of default on the part of the original servicer.

The Issuer

The underlying issuer (or conduit or special purpose vehicle) must be structured to protect both the asset pool and the claims of the investors. If the originator in the transaction is eligible to seek protection under bankruptcy laws, such protection will prohibit anyone from taking action against the property of the originator. If the individual assets in the asset pool are deemed to be property of the originator, then the collateral for the asset-backed security is jeopardized.

Also, in some cases, bankruptcy procedures require a secured creditor to exchange the original collateral for another form of collateral. For example, a lien on liquid assets, such as receivables, may be replaced by a lien on plant and equipment. Such a substitution will significantly alter the cash flows that are generated by the asset pool – plant and equipment generate no contractual cash flows. Such a substitution would cause the asset-backed security to default. Even if receivables are exchanged for receivables, the credit quality of the asset pool could be materially affected by the substitution, again exposing investors to credit risk.

For these reasons, the issuer must be structured in a way that creates a bankruptcy-remote entity, either in the form of a trust, corporation, or partnership. The characteristics that cause the issuer to be bankruptcy-remote will be contained in the entity's by-laws. In addition, these provisions should also be included in the documentation for the asset-backed securities so that investors have a full appreciation of the protective covenants. Specifically, the issuer must:

- limit its activities to the asset-backed securities transaction in question;
- engage in no other business;
- be prohibited from incurring any debt other than that associated with the asset-backed security issue – the only exception to debt issuance that is acceptable is the issuance of debt that is fully subordinated to the asset-backed security, nonrecourse in nature, payable only from excess cash, and may not constitute a claim enforceable against the issuer in a bankruptcy proceeding;
- be prohibited from merging or consolidating with any other entity, unless the surviving entity is also bankruptcy-remote.

Issuers are very often subsidiaries of originators.[9] In the event of bankruptcy of the originator, it is critical that the issuer not be consolidated with the parent in the bankruptcy proceeding. If consolidation does occur, the issue of substitution of collateral and other problematic situations will jeopardize the security of investors. In deciding whether a consolidation is reasonable, courts will generally consider factors such as the degree of difficulty in segregating the assets and liabilities of the two entities, the presence or absence of consolidated financial statements, commingling of assets and business functions, and the extent to which ownership and other interest is shared between the issuer (subsidiary) and the originator (parent). To perfect a separation of the originator and the issuer, the following should be considered:

- separate officers and directors
- separate books and records
- periodic and regular meetings of the board of directors of the issuer

---

[9] The other possibility is that the issuer would be a subsidiary of the investment banker, in which case it is referred to as an "orphan subsidiary."

- separate offices
- separate bank accounts
- payment of issuer's expenses by the issuer (not by the originator)
- no benefit to issuer from intercompany guarantees
- statement and warranty on the part of the originator that it is not responsible for debts of the issuer.

Another area that must be addressed in maintaining the bankruptcy-remote status for the issuer is the integrity of the transfer of title of individual assets in the asset pool. The transfer must be a "true sale." This status is not necessarily guaranteed simply because there is a purchase and sale agreement between the issuer and the originator. In some cases, courts may decide that the transfer of the assets to the issuer was a collateralized borrowing on the part of the parent. In this case, the assets would be considered part of the property of the originator and subject to bankruptcy proceedings for the originator. There are some guidelines that can assist in the establishment of an issuer such that this circumstance becomes less likely.

- Does the issuer have the right of recourse to other assets of the originator if the individual assets in the asset pool do not provide sufficient cash flow?
- Do the issuer's rights in the property end if the receivables or loans are paid with funds from another source?
- Must the issuer account to the originator for any cash flows received from the pool assets if these amounts exceed the amount of the obligation at the time that the pool is formed and transferred?
- Does the language in the purchase and sale document indicate an intention to make an assignment rather than a sale?
- Does the sale discharge an obligation of the originator?

Because these are highly technical issues, it is necessary to seek a legal opinion concerning establishment of an effective legal transfer of assets. The ability to demonstrate protection from consolidation with the originator and avoidance of a failed legal transfer of assets are directly related to the protection of investors and the ability to establish a credit rating based on the assets in the pool.

The Trustee

Like the servicer, the *trustee* must demonstrate the ability to perform its responsibilities over the term of the asset-backed security. The responsibilities of the trustee include management of trust funds and accounts, tracking payment streams on a monthly or quarterly basis, reporting to investors and other concerned entities on a monthly or quarterly basis, and the ability to act as a servicer in the event that the originally designated servicer fails to fulfill its responsibilities.

While the trustee has less direct contact with the pool assets or the cash flows from the assets, the inability of the trustee to perform its duties may delay payments. The confidence in the trustee to fulfill these duties can perhaps best be established by assigning a trustee that has an investment grade credit rating.[10] Another provision in the documentation for the asset-backed security that will add confidence in the structure is provision for a substitute trustee in the event that the original trustee is unable to perform its functions. Of course, the experience of a trustee in handling such issues is also an important element in the evaluation of trustee credit risk.

Credit Enhancement

Credit enhancement can be provided for the issue either through external means or by specific internal structures. Bank letters of credit and private insurance are the most common external means of credit enhancement. The general rule is that the credit enhancer should have a credit rating that is no lower than the credit rating of the asset-backed security without credit enhancement. This is the theory of the "weakest link" which suggests that the credit is only as strong as the credit of the weakest participant in the structure.

---

[10] Recall that the trustee is typically a bank with capital in excess of $500 million.

In many cases, external credit support is provided not for the entire amount of the asset pool, but instead for the anticipated loss or maximum tolerable loss of the asset pool. If the asset pool is amortizing, as is true with mortgage loans, the credit enhancement may "step down" – or decrease – as the unpaid balance of the pool assets declines. Some transactions with step-down provisions permit the step-down only in the event that the actual loss experience, perhaps during the first five years, is within predetermined limits.

Internal methods of credit enhancement include (1) cash collateral or reserve accounts and (2) senior-subordinated structures. *Reserve accounts* are established, in some cases, in lieu of letters of credit. In such a case, a commercial bank typically lends funds to the issuer on behalf of the investors and the cash is held in liquid, investment grade instruments that is available to cover portfolio delinquencies and losses. The types of investments that are appropriate for these funds are:

- Government obligations, obligations guaranteed by the government, or federal agency securities;
- Demand deposits, time deposits, or certificates of deposit from a bank or other equivalent depository institution with a high, investment grade credit rating;
- Bankers' acceptances from similarly rated institutions;
- Commercial paper with top credit ratings;
- Money market funds with top credit ratings, specifically those that invest in instruments as indicated above.

The *senior-subordinated structure* is an example of the way pay-through bonds provide credit protection for certain tranches. There are basically four types of senior-subordinated structures that provide credit protection for the senior instruments – fast pay/slow pay, shifting interest, fixed amount, and step-down mechanisms.

Fast pay/slow pay is a structure in which 100 percent of all principal collections, including prepayments, is paid to the senior class investors. In this structure, the payback to the senior certificate holders is accelerated, shortening the length of time that the certificate holder is exposed to credit and other risks.

In a *shifting interest* transaction, some payments can be allocated to the subordinated tranche(s) earlier than would otherwise be the case. In this situation, however, the senior certificate holders must receive all cash flows to which they are contractually entitled before the subordinated certificate holders receive any cash distribution. To the extent that subordinated certificate holders receive payments, the degree of internal credit support is reduced.

An alternative structure is the *fixed amount* arrangement. In this case, the subordinated certificates are obligated to absorb a specified percentage of the senior investors exposure in terms of loss. Beyond this specified loss amount, the subordinated certificate holders are not obligated to absorb additional losses that may occur.

As noted above in terms of external credit support, the internal *step-down* mechanism is appropriate for amortizing assets, such as mortgage loans, home equity loans, and manufactured housing loans. For example, a subordinated class of certificates may absorb all the losses that are incurred by a senior class of certificates until certain thresholds are reached.

For example, consider a structure in which the senior certificates represent claims on 85 percent of the original amount of the asset pool, with subordinated certificates representing the remaining 15 percent. A declining subordination may require that the subordinated certificates absorb losses sustained by the senior class until the senior class is amortized down to 70 percent of the unpaid mortgage balance. At this point, the two classes of certificates absorb losses based on some other formula, perhaps in proportional shares.

Credit enhancements are varied and continue to evolve as the structure of asset-backed securities continues to evolve. The best structures will include a combination of both external and internal credit support.

CHAPTER 3

COMPUTING THE COST OF CAPITAL

Introduction

■

Conditions that Influence the Cost of Capital

■

Sources of Information for the Cost of Capital

■

Bishop Manufacturing and the Book Value of Capital

■

The Market Value of Capital

■

The Cost of Capital for Bishop Manufacturing Company

INTRODUCTION

The cost of capital is the minimum required rate of return that a project must earn in order to be accepted. The most appropriate rate for this purpose is the weighted average cost of capital (WACC) because this rate satisfies all suppliers of capital. The WACC will depend on general market conditions as well as the market's perception of the risk of the issuing company.

3

FIGURE 3.1

Considerations in Determining the Required Rate of Return

- Interest rate environment

- Risk

- Financial market conditions

- Suppliers of capital

CONDITIONS THAT INFLUENCE THE COST OF CAPITAL

Figure 3.1 outlines the important factors that help determine the appropriate cost of capital. The first is the *interest rate environment*. Generally, if interest rates are relatively high, the required rate of return for projects will also be relatively high. Conversely, in more moderate interest rate environments, the required rate of return will be lower.

The second factor is *risk*. Risk is not a function of market conditions, as is the interest rate environment, but reflects the characteristics of a specific firm or the industry in which it operates. Risk may be uncertainty of cash flow, of sales market, of raw materials supplies, or any number of other considerations. Generally, higher risk projects require a higher minimum required rate of return.[1]

The third factor is *financial market conditions*. Long-term projects are financed with long-term sources of financing. When the stock market is weak and stock is selling at relatively low multiples of earnings, it may not be feasible to issue equity securities to finance projects because low prices imply that stock holders require relatively high rates of return.[2] Likewise, when interest rates are high, issuing bonds will obligate the firm to relatively high interest payments. Market conditions can affect not only the timing of the fund raising, but also the mix of funds.

As explained in Chapter 1, *suppliers of capital* are entities that invest long-term funds in the corporation. Suppliers of capital include bondholders, mortgage lenders, preferred stock shareholders, and common stock shareholders. Common stock shareholders require a higher rate of return than do bond holders. Thus, to the extent that a project is financed primarily through equity, the weighted average cost of capital will be higher. Lower costs of funds will result when a higher mix of debt is included in the funding base.

---

[1] See also Chapter 2 for a discussion of bond ratings as a measurement of risk and securitization as a method for managing risk.

[2] The valuation models for stocks and bonds are explained later in the chapter.

SOURCES OF INFORMATION FOR THE COST OF CAPITAL

In determining its cost of capital, a firm may refer to several sources of information, as indicated in Figure 3.2. These include investment bankers, the securities of the firm that are currently outstanding, and securities of other firms.

3

FIGURE 3.2
Information Sources
■ Investment bankers
■ Securities of own firm
■ Securities of other firms

Investment bankers offer services for corporations in issuing new securities, including advice as to the correct mix of debt and equity, the structure of an issue (for example, offering price for stock, coupon rate for bonds, conventional versus asset-backed securities), and the appropriate timing of the issue. Investment bankers also offer information about financial market conditions.

The *securities of the firm* that are already outstanding also provide important information to the issuing firm. For example, if the firm's bonds are selling to yield a specific rate of return, this information gives the issuing firm an indication of the likely receptiveness of the market to new bonds. If the stock of the firm is selling at a relatively high level, as compared to earnings, this would suggest that the market is generally receptive to new stock issued by the firm. The trading of the firm's own securities and the *securities of other firms* among investors takes place in the secondary market.[3] Thus, the secondary market is an important source of information for new issues and is, in a sense, the way issuing firms decide the timing for new issues.

---

[3] Securities are issued for the first time in *primary securities markets*. Once issued, securities trade among investors in *secondary securities markets*.

BISHOP MANUFACTURING AND THE BOOK VALUE OF CAPITAL

Figure 3.3 is the balance sheet as of December 31, 1999 for Bishop Manufacturing, a hypothetical industrial firm. Bishop has total assets of $515 million, of which $230 million is financed with liabilities and $285 million with equity. However, the concept of capital does not include all categories in the liabilities. *Capital* is sources of permanent financing, excluding short-term liabilities. Thus, for Bishop Manu-facturing, the book value of capital will include long-term debt, preferred stock, com-mon stock, and retained earnings – a total book value of $435 million. These components only are considered in computing the weighted average cost of capital.

FIGURE 3.3

Bishop Manufacturing Co., Consolidated Balance Sheet, December 31, 1999, in Millions of Dollars

Assets			Liabilities	
Cash		$ 50	Accounts payable	$ 10
			Accrued expenses	5
Accounts receivable		125	Notes payable	65
			Long-term debt	150
Inventory		75	Total liabilities	230
Fixed assets:			**Equity**	
Land	$100			
Buildings	130		Preferred stock	50
Equipment	200		Common stock	85
	430		Retained earnings	150
Acc. deprec.	(165)		Total equity	285
Net fixed assets		265		
			Total liabilities	
Total assets		$515	& equity	$515

FIGURE 3.4

Weighted Average Cost of Capital

$$\text{WACC} = k_a = w_\text{D} k_\text{D} (1 - t) + w_p k_p + w_\text{E} k_\text{E}$$

where WACC $= k_a$ = weighted average cost of capital
w_D = percent of total capital composed of debt
w_p = percent of total capital composed of preferred stock
w_E = percent of total capital composed of common equity
k_D = before-tax cost of debt
k_p = cost of preferred stock
k_E = cost of common equity
t = tax rate

3

Figure 3.4 illustrates the calculation of the weighted average cost of capital or WACC. Notice that there are three *components of capital* – debt, preferred stock, and common equity and that each is assigned a weight. The *weight of a component* of capital, denoted by the variable w, corresponds to the share of total capital which that component represents. Note that the weights are based on the amount of *capital*, not the total amount of liabilities and equity. The *component cost* of either debt, preferred stock, or common equity is indicated by the variable k and identified with a distinguishing subscript.

In addition, the cost of debt is adjusted for taxes. This adjustment for taxes [multiplication $(1 - t)$] is necessary because interest expense is tax-deductible. Since the firm pays 100 percent of interest expense (interest expense multiplied by 1) and t percent is deducted from taxable income (interest expense multiplied by t), the net cost to the firm is $k_\text{D}(1 - t)$. When each component cost is weighted by its respective share of total capital (its weight), and these terms are summed, the result is the weighted average cost of capital, *WACC*.

FIGURE 3.5

Bishop Manufacturing Co., Weighted Average Cost of Capital, Calculating the Weights Using Book Value

$$w_D = 150/435 = 0.345$$
$$w_p = 50/435 = 0.115$$
$$w_E = 235/435 = 0.540$$

Figure 3.5 uses the concept of weighted average cost of capital in the case of Bishop Manufacturing. Since the total amount of capital is \$435 million, the weight of debt, w_D, is 0.345 or $\dfrac{150}{435}$. Likewise, the weights of preferred stock, w_p, and equity, w_E, are 0.115 and 0.540, respectively. Notice that the sum of these weights is 1.0, as will always be the case.

THE MARKET VALUE OF CAPITAL

The consolidated balance sheet of Bishop Manufacturing was useful in relating the concept of capital to the balance sheet. However, the more relevant concept of capital is *market value* rather than book value. This is true because decisions to raise capital (debt or equity) are made in anticipation of investing in new projects (assets). The funding for these new projects will be obtained in long-term financial markets. Thus, the market values of the firm's current debt and equity, as well as its future issuances of debt and equity, are relevant. These market values can be explained in the context of the principles of pricing:

- bonds
- preferred stock
- common stock.

Bond Pricing

The value of a bond is the present value of the future cash flows associated with the bond.[4] Figure 3.6 illustrates that a bond represents two types of cash flows. The first form of cash flow associated with a bond is its *maturity value* (M), or the lump sum amount that the issuer promises to pay when the bond matures. The maturity value may also be referred to as the *par value* or *face value*. Typically, corporate bonds have a maturity value of $1,000 each.

The second form of cash flow associated with a bond is a stream of *interest payments*. The amount and timing of these (usually predetermined)

FIGURE 3.6

Bond Pricing

$$P_o = I\ (PVIFA_{k,n}) + M\ (PVIF_{k,n})$$

where P_o = market value or price of a debt security
  M = maturity value
  = face value
  = par value
  CR = coupon rate
  = percent of face value paid each year as interest
  m = number of times per year interest is paid
  I = dollar amount of interest paid each period
  = $(CR)(M)/m$
  k = required rate of return per period
  n = number of periods remaining before bond matures
  $PVIFA_{k,n}$ = present value interest factor of an annuity
    (see Appendix B)
  $PVIF_{k,n}$ = present value interest factor of a single amount
    (see Appendix B)

---

[4] See Appendix B for time value of money factors.

interest payments are described in the bond's *indenture*.[5] The amount of each interest payment is determined by the bond's maturity value (M), coupon rate (CR), and the number of times per year that interest is paid (*m*). The product of M and CR is the dollar amount of interest paid each year. When this amount is divided by *m*, the result is a dollar amount of interest paid each period.

The market value of a bond is the present value of maturity value and interest payments, discounted at the appropriate market rate of return. Since the maturity value is a single amount and the interest payments are an annuity, valuation of cash flows is accomplished in two steps. While the maturity value is multiplied by the appropriate present value interest factor of a single amount, the interest payment amount is multiplied by the appropriate present value interest factor of an annuity.

FIGURE 3.7

Examples of Bond Pricing

Example 1

Given: M = $1,000, CR = 0.095, m = 2, required rate of return = 0.08,
     years to maturity = 5

P_o = 47.50 $(PVIFA_{0.04,10})$ + 1,000 $(PVIF_{0.04,10})$

  = 47.50 (8.1109) + 1,000(0.6756)

  = 385.27 + 675.60

  = 1060.87

Example 2

Given: M = $1,000, CR = 0.055, m = 2, required rate of return = 0.08,
     years to maturity = 5

P_o = 27.50 $(PVIFA_{0.04,10})$ + 1,000 $(PVIF_{0.04,10})$

  = 27.50 (8.1109) + 1,000(0.6756)

  = 223.05 + 675.60

  = 898.65

---

[5] A bond indenture is the contract between the bond issuer and the bondholder. All terms and conditions, including restrictive covenants (restrictions of action on the part of the bond issuer) and default provisions, are included.

Premium Bonds

Figure 3.7 shows the calculation of the market value for two sample bonds. The first bond has a maturity value of $1,000 and a coupon rate of 9.5 percent, paid semiannually. These means that $47.50 is paid at the end of each six-month period over the life of the bond. Since the bond has five years to maturity, there will be ten payments of $47.50 before the $1,000 maturity value is paid by the bond issuer. The amount and timing of these payments are established at the time of bond issuance, documented in the indenture, and will not change.

The present value of these payments will vary as market interest rates vary. In this instance, the required rate of return is assumed to be 8 percent per year, or 4 percent each six-month period. The market value of this bond ($1,060.87) exceeds its maturity value ($1,000). This result is obtained because the coupon rate (9.5 percent) exceeds the required return of 8 percent. As a result, investors are willing to pay a *premium* for the bond.

Discount Bonds

The second example in Figure 3.7 is similar to the first, with one exception. The coupon rate of the second bond is 5.5 percent, resulting in semi-annual payments of $27.50. Because this is a smaller interest payment (as compared to the first bond in the exhibit) over the same period of time at the same market rate of return, the present value of the second bond is lower. In fact, the market value ($898.65) is below the maturity value (1,000), again, because of the relationship between the coupon rate and the required return. In this case, the coupon rate (5.5 percent) is less than the required return (8 percent), causing the bond to sell at a *discount*.

Yield to Maturity

Notice that in the first and second examples in Figure 3.7, the value of a bond depends on the *required market rate of return*, which will vary with the interest rate environment. When the general level of interest rates declines, the required return will also decline. Should interest rates increase generally, the required return for a bond will also increase. All other things being equal, it is the market rate of return that determines the bond's price after issuance (in the secondary market), because all other terms of the bond are fixed by provisions in the indenture.

Viewing the bond pricing formula in Figure 3.6 as the bond valuation formula, it is possible to derive the *expected return* of a bond. The expected return of a bond is that rate which will *cause the present value of the future interest payments* and *maturity value* (documented in the indenture) *to exactly equal the current market price (objectively observed in the secondary market)*. This concept of expected return is the same for any financial instrument. The expected return is that rate which will cause the present value of future cash flows (in any form) to exactly equal the market price.

FIGURE 3.8

Yield to Maturity

YTM = Rate which causes the present value of future cash flows to exactly equal the market price

$$YTM = \frac{\left[I + \dfrac{(M - P_o)}{n} \right]}{\left[\dfrac{M + 2(P_o)}{3} \right]}$$

where YTM = annual or periodic expected rate of return on a debt security

= yield to maturity

I = annual or periodic interest payment

P_o = market value or price

M = maturity value

n = number of years or periods

In the case of a bond, the expected rate of return is referred to as the bond's *yield to maturity* (YTM). Figure 3.8 contains a yield to maturity (YTM) approximation, with an average annual return to a bondholder in the numerator and the average investment by a bondholder in the denominator.

The annual interest payments and the average annual capital gain are in the *numerator* of the YTM approximation. The interest payment is defined in the same way as the interest payment in Figure 3.8. The total capital gain or loss is the difference between the current market value of the bond and the future payoff, or maturity value. This total capital gain is divided by the number of years or periods that remain in the useful life of a bond. This again reflects the fact that a bondholder receives two forms of income or return – interest paid by the bond issuer and the increase or decrease in the value of the bond over time.

The *denominator* of the YTM approximation represents an average investment and is the simple average of three values – the maturity value and twice the current market price. When the sum of these three values is divided by 3, an average investment is the result. Again, the YTM approximation is an average annual income as a percentage of an average investment. The YTM is the market's assessment of the cost of debt.

Bishop Manufacturing Company Bonds

In the case of Bishop Manufacturing, the face value of bonds outstanding is $150 million – 150,000 bonds at a face value of $1,000 each (see Figure 3.3). Figure 3.9 provides additional information about these bonds. The current market price of these bonds is $1,020 each. The coupon rate is 7.5 percent, paid semiannually, and the bonds mature in ten years.

In the numerator of the YTM computation, the semiannual interest payments and average capital gain per six-month period are provided – a total of $36.50 (Figure 3.9). The denominator includes the average investment of $1,013.33. The result is an approximate semiannual YTM of 3.602 percent. Multiplying this result by 2 results in an approximate annual YTM of 7.204 percent.[6] This is the cost of debt that is relevant for Bishop Manufacturing in computing its weighted average cost of capital. Notice that the relevant cost of debt is *not* 7.5 percent, the coupon rate, but is instead the market-driven yield to maturity.

FIGURE 3.9

Bishop Manufacturing Co., Bonds Outstanding, Yield to Maturity

Given: M = \$1,000, P_0 = \$1,020, CR = 0.075, m = 2, years to maturity = 10, number of bonds outstanding = 150,000

$$YTM = \frac{\left[I + \dfrac{(M - P_0)}{n} \right]}{\left[\dfrac{M + 2(P_0)}{3} \right]}$$

$$YTM = \frac{\left[37.50 + \dfrac{(1,000 - 1,020)}{20} \right]}{\left[\dfrac{1,000 + 2\,(1,020)}{3} \right]}$$

$$= \frac{[37.50 - 1]}{[1,013.3333]}$$

$$= 0.03602$$

$$= \text{semiannual YTM}$$

$$\text{annual YTM} = (2)(0.03602)$$

$$= 0.07204$$

---

[6] The actual semiannual YTM is 3.509 percent and the annual YTM 7.018 percent. This result may be obtained by using a handheld financial calculator. Such calculators are programmed to use a trial-and-error approach until arriving at the rate that will cause the present value of future cash flows to exactly equal the market price.

Pricing Preferred Stock

The value of preferred stock is also based on the present value of future cash flows. The difference is that preferred stock does not have a maturity date or maturity value.[7] Preferred stock is a claim on the firm for an indefinite period of time, with fixed dividend payments. In other words, preferred stock dividends represent an annuity that does not end, or a *perpetuity*. Figure 3.10 illustrates the valuation of preferred stock. The value of a perpetuity of level dividends, each in the amount of D_1, is the amount of the next dividend divided by the required rate of return.[8]

3

FIGURE 3.10

Pricing Preferred Stock

$$P_o = \frac{D_1}{k}$$

where P_o = market value or price
D_1 = dividend per share next period
k = required return

---

[7] In a few rare exceptions, firms (notably, financial institutions) may issue limited life preferred stock, with a stated maturity date.

[8] In general, the value of a perpetuity is the amount of the level payment divided by the required return.

FIGURE 3.11

Examples of Preferred Stock Pricing

Example 1

Given: $D_1 = \$5$, $k = 0.06$

$$P_o = \frac{5}{0.06}$$

$$= \underline{\underline{83.33}}$$

Example 2

Given: Par value = $20, Dividend = 5%, $k = 0.07$

$$P_o = \frac{20(0.05)}{0.07}$$

$$= \frac{1}{0.07}$$

$$= \underline{\underline{14.29}}$$

Stated Dividends

Figure 3.11 provides two examples of preferred stock pricing. In the first example, the dividend that is paid each year is specified at $5 per year. The minimum required return for this stock, based on its risk and current market conditions, is 6 percent. Each share of preferred stock in the first example has a market value of $83.33.

Stated Dividend Rate

The second example of preferred stock in Figure 3.11 has a *stated* or *par value* of $20. In this case, the annual dividend is specified as 5 percent of the par value or $1 per share. Since the required rate of return is 7 percent, the market value of this preferred stock is $14.29 per share. In general, preferred stock dividends will be stated either as a fixed dollar amount or as a fixed percentage of par value.

FIGURE 3.12

Bishop Manufacturing Co., Preferred Stock Outstanding, Required Return

Given: Par value = \$25, Dividend = 8%, P_o = \$20, number of shares
outstanding = 2 million

$$P_o = \frac{D_1}{k}$$

$$k = \frac{D_1}{P_o}$$

$$= \frac{25\,(0.08)}{20}$$

$$= \frac{2}{20}$$

$$= \underline{\underline{0.10}}$$

Bishop Manufacturing Company Preferred Stock

In the case of Bishop Manufacturing, the preferred stock outstanding is
\$50 million (see Figure 3.3). Each share has a par value of \$25 so that the
2 million shares that are outstanding represent a total book value of \$50
million as shown in Figure 3.12. The dividend rate for this preferred stock
is 8 percent, a contractual percentage of par value that will be paid each
year as dividends on the stock. However, the current market value of the
stock is \$20 per share. Since the stock is not selling at the par value it can
be inferred that the market rate of return differs from the dividend rate of
8 percent.

Determining the *market rate of return* of the preferred stock is similar to
finding the yield to maturity of a bond. The process involves identifying
the correct valuation formula, substituting all known values (the current
market value and the relevant cash flow stream), and solving for k. When
this is done in the case of the preferred stock of Bishop Manufacturing,
the result is a 10 percent rate of return on the preferred stock (Figure 3.12).
This is the rate of return that should be used in calculating the cost of preferred stock capital for the company.

Pricing Common Stock

In the case of common stock, the dividend stream is not constant, as is true with preferred stock. For stock with dividends that are expected to grow at some fairly constant rate, the dividend stream can be conceptualized as a stream of constantly growing cash flows. Under this assumption, the stream of perpetually growing dividends is valued using the formula in Figure 3.13.[9]

FIGURE 3.13

Pricing Common Stock

$$P_o = \frac{D_1}{k - g}$$

where P_o = market value or price

D_1 = dividend per share next period

k = required return

g = anticipated growth rate of earnings, dividends, and stock price

---

The valuation of common stock (assuming a constant growth rate of dividends, earnings, assets, and stock price) depends on the next anticipated dividend, the required return, and the growth rate. As shown in Figure 3.13, under the constant growth assumption, the value of a share of stock at the current time (or at any point of valuation on the time line) is the projected dividend for next year (or the year subsequent to the point of valuation) divided by the difference between the required return and the constant growth rate.

---

[9] The model in Figure 3.13 is known as the Gordon Constant Growth model. It is based on the assumption that each successive dividend will grow at a constant rate of growth over the previous dividend. This amounts to a geometric progression in which the value of each successive term increases by the same multiplicative factor. This geometric progression converges to the closed form equation given in Figure 3.13.

FIGURE 3.14

Examples of Common Stock Pricing

Example 1

Given: $D_1 = \$2.50$, $g = 0.05$, $k = 0.15$

$$P_o = \left[\frac{2.50}{0.15 - 0.05} \right]$$

$$= \left[\frac{2.50}{0.10} \right]$$

$$= \underline{\underline{25}}$$

Example 2

Given: $D_o = \$3$, $g = 0.05$, $k = 0.18$

$$P_o = \left[\frac{3(1.05)}{0.18 - 0.05} \right]$$

$$= \left[\frac{3.15}{0.13} \right]$$

$$= \underline{\underline{24.23}}$$

3

Common Stock Examples

Figure 3.14 illustrates this process. In Example 1 of the figure, the projected dividend per share for next year is $2.50. The dividends are growing (and are anticipated to continue to grow) at the rate of 5 percent per year. The required return on a stock is 15 percent. Substituting these values, the market value is $25 per share.

In the second example, the current dividend, that is, the dividend most recently received, is $3 per share and the growth rate is 5 percent. Next year's dividend will not be $3 but $3.15 [$3(1.05)]. This $3.15 is then capitalized at a 13 percent rate, the difference between the required return of 18 percent and the expected growth rate of 5 percent. The market value of a share of this stock is $24.23.

FIGURE 3.15

Bishop Manufacturing Co., Common Stock Outstanding, Required Return

Given: $D_o = \$1.51$, $g = 0.07$, $P_o = \$20.25$, number of shares outstanding = 12 million

$$P_o = \frac{D_1}{k - g}$$

$$P_o (k - g) = D_1$$

$$k - g = \frac{D_1}{P_o}$$

$$k = \frac{D_1}{P_o} + g$$

$$= \left[\frac{1.51(1.07)}{20.25} \right] + 0.07$$

$$= \left[\frac{1.62}{20.25} \right] + 0.07$$

$$= 0.08 + 0.07$$

$$= \underline{\underline{0.15}}$$

Bishop Manufacturing Company Common Stock

Bishop Manufacturing has a total of 12 million shares of common stock outstanding. Figure 3.15 gives additional information about this stock. The dividend that was most recently paid is $1.51 per share. The growth rate of dividends and stock price is 7 percent. Accordingly, Bishop's projected dividend next year is $1.62 per share.

Since the current stock price is known ($20.25 per share) and the dividend stream is anticipated to grow at 7 percent, it is possible to determine the rate of return for a shareholder. Once again, the appropriate valuation formula is determined, all known variables are substituted, and the equation is solved for the variable k. Using the stock valuation model in Figure 3.13, the

return to a shareholder is the sum of (1) dividend yield, $\dfrac{D_1}{P_0}$, and (2)
percentage change in price, g. The dividend yield for Bishop Manufacturing
stock is 8 percent $\left(\dfrac{\$1.62}{\$20.25}\right)$ and the growth rate is 7 percent so that a
Bishop shareholder can expect a total rate of return of 15 percent. In
estimating the weighted average cost of capital, Bishop should use this 15
percent as the cost of equity funds.

3

THE COST OF CAPITAL FOR BISHOP MANUFACTURING COMPANY

It is now possible to evaluate the market value of the capital of Bishop
Manufacturing and its weighted average cost of capital on a market-value
basis.

FIGURE 3.16

Bishop Manufacturing Co., Total Capital and Weights Using Market Value

	Price[1]	# O/S[2]	Market value[3]	Weight[4]
Bonds	$1,020	150,000	$153	0.351
Preferred stock	$20	2 million	$40	0.092
Common stock	$20.25	12 million	$243	0.557
			$436	1.000

[1] Market value per bond or per share of stock.
[2] Number of bonds or shares of stock outstanding.
[3] Price multiplied by number outstanding, in millions of dollars.
[4] Market value of bonds or stock divided by total market value.

The cost of capital is based on the following three components and their costs:

- Debt (Figure 3.9)
- Preferred stock (Figure 3.12)
- Common stock (Figure 3.15).

Market Value of Capital

Figure 3.16 contains the three components of the capital structure of Bishop Manufacturing. The unit market value of each instrument (bond or share) is indicated along with the number outstanding. When the unit price and the number of units outstanding are multiplied, the result is the total market value – $153 million in bonds, $40 million in preferred stock, and $243 million in common stock. The grand total of $436 million represents the market value of capital for Bishop Manufacturing. Using these components and the grand total, the recomputed weights of components of capital are 0.351 for bonds, and 0.092 and 0.557 for preferred and common stock, respectively. Notice, once again, that the weights sum to 1.

Weighted Average Cost of Capital

These component costs and these new market-value weights are combined in Figure 3.17 to compute the weighted average cost of capital of Bishop Manufacturing. Assuming a 34 percent tax rate, the weighted average cost of capital is 10.944 percent.

FIGURE 3.17

Bishop Manufacturing Co., Weighted Average Cost of Capital Using Market Value

$$\begin{aligned}
\text{WACC} &= k_a = w_D k_D (1 - t) + w_p k_p + w_E k_E \\
&= 0.351(0.07204)(1 - 0.34) + 0.092(0.10) + 0.557(0.15) \\
&= 0.01669 + 0.00920 + 0.08355 \\
&= 0.10944
\end{aligned}$$

This market-value approach is the best method for determining the WACC for a firm. It is the appropriate rate of return to use for capital budgeting purposes and also is referred to as *the minimum required rate of return, the opportunity cost of capital*, or *the hurdle rate*. This is the (required) rate of return that should be used to compute net present values or to compare to the internal rates of return (expected return) of proposed investment projects.[10]

3

---

[10] The *net present value* of a project is the difference between the value of the project and the cost of the project. A project is acceptable when the value of a project equals or exceeds its cost. The net present value assumes a minimum required rate of return – the weighted average cost of capital. The *internal rate of return* is the expected return of a project – the rate that causes the present value of the future cash flows to exactly equal the cost. A project is acceptable when the internal rate of return equals or exceeds the cost of capital.

CHAPTER 4

WHEN THE COST OF CAPITAL CHANGES

Introduction

■

The WACC Schedule

■

The Investment Opportunity Schedule

■

The Optimal Capital Budget

■

A Dynamic Process

INTRODUCTION

The weighted average cost of capital or WACC – in market value terms, as discussed in Chapter 3 – is the appropriate measure of the minimum required rate of return for investment projects by a firm. However, whenever the cost of one of the components changes, the WACC will change. Accordingly, the cost of capital should be thought of as a *WACC schedule*, rather than a single point estimate.

Given that WACC changes, the acceptability of potential investment projects also changes. The process of (1) ranking investment projects and (2) identifying the appropriate cost of capital for each yields the optimal combination of investment projects. The *optimal capital budget* is the sum of required initial investments for those projects with expected returns that exceed their cost of capital.

THE WACC SCHEDULE

A firm's cost of capital will be stable over certain ranges of new securities issuances and corresponding asset investments. However, as the amount of required capital increases, the risk of the firm also increases.

Consider a simple example. Suppose that a firm with $100 million in assets seeks to raise $10 million in new capital. The perception of the financial markets may be that the risk associated with this level of new capital investment is relatively low. However, if the same firm endeavors to acquire another company with an acquisition cost of $200 million, issuing new securities to finance the acquisition, the market's perception of the risk of this firm will increase considerably. The funds raised in the second situation will be associated with much higher costs. Thus, a firm's cost of capital will be stable over some relevant range, but will be subject to increases as the amount of new capital increases.

Securities Flotation Costs and the Cost of Capital

Whenever a firm issues new securities, it will incur costs directly associated with issuance. These costs are commonly referred to as *flotation costs* and they are composed of a number of elements. The first element is the *out-of-pocket cost* that is associated with issuing new securities, including preparing and duplicating a prospectus to be approved by the Securities and Exchange Commission and to be distributed to the investing public. The prospectus describes the issuing company in detail and the planned use of the proceeds of the securities issue. Also, legal and auditing fees are incurred because legal opinions and statements by external auditors must be included in the prospectus. The legal opinions address the possibility of future liabilities associated with lawsuits and other legal proceedings. The auditor's work includes addressing the reasonableness of the financial statements included in the prospectus.

Flotation cost also includes *compensation to the underwriters*. When an investment banker lead-manages an underwriting of new securities, it will often do so under what is referred to as a firm commitment. In this arrangement, an investment banker guarantees the sale of the new securities at a specified price. That is, the issuing company is guaranteed to receive specified proceeds from the issuance of the securities. It is then the responsibility of the lead underwriter and the syndicate of other investment bankers to sell the new securities to the investing public. In exchange for accepting this risk, the underwriter and syndicate participants receive compensation in the form of the *underwriters discount* – the difference between the price at which the securities are sold to the public and the price that is paid to the issuing company.

The third type of flotation cost is *price dilution*. A firm is often required to offer new stock at a lower price than currently outstanding shares in order to sell the entire issue. This is true even if the new capital will be invested in a project that actually increases the wealth of shareholders. Information asymmetries suggest that shareholders initially may not fully appreciate the value associated with new projects. On the surface, increasing the number of shares outstanding appears to reduce the value of each share. In such cases, new stock will be issued at a price at or below (generally below) the current market price.

Taken together, out-of-pocket costs, compensation to underwriters, and price dilution constitute flotation cost, which is often expressed as a percentage of the current market price. In Figure 4.1 the flotation cost is denoted by the variable F.

FIGURE 4.1

Component Costs of Capital, Flotation Costs

Preferred stock

$$k_p = \frac{D_1}{P_o(1 - F)}$$

Retained earnings

$$k_{R/E} = \frac{D_1}{P_o} + g$$

Common stock

$$k_{C/S} = \frac{D_1}{P_o(I - F)} + g$$

Note:

F = flotation cost

= percentage of price that represents total cost of floating a new issue

---

In the case of *preferred stock*, another component cost of capital is the dividend yield as noted in Chapter 3 (Figure 3.12). However, the stock price in the denominator of the dividend yield must be adjusted for the payment of flotation costs. The adjusted cost of preferred stock is indicated as the first of the three equations in Figure 4.1.

To the extent that a firm does not plan to pay dividends in the future, *future retained earnings* may be used for future investment in capital projects. Notice that only *future* retained earnings may be targeted for future investment. While there is no flotation cost associated with the use of future retained earnings, the use of future earnings can be justified only if the future earnings are invested in projects that will earn for common shareholders at least the rate of return that they currently earn. If future earnings cannot be so invested, they should be paid as dividends to allow shareholders to invest – individually – in their next best investment alternatives. This means that the cost of using future retained earnings is the sum of the dividend yield and growth rate as described in Chapter 3 (Figure 3.15). The cost of retained earnings is the second of the three equations in Figure 4.1.

In the case of *new common stock*, issuance will involve flotation costs. The required return for new common stock then is higher than the required return for using future retained earnings because flotation cost must be covered as well as shareholders' return. The proceeds of common stock issuance will be net of flotation costs. This adjustment is shown in the third equation in Figure 4.1 and represents the minimum required rate of return for new common stock.

Constructing a WACC Schedule

All component costs – debt, preferred stock, and common stock – will be stable as long as flotation cost is constant and there are no other changes in component cost. Should flotation cost of one of the three components change or the cost of debt change, the weighted average cost of capital will also change. Because of these dynamics, it is necessary to construct a WACC schedule.

Also, the use of future projected retained earnings suggests one required return for common equity, at least until the future retained earnings are exhausted. When the future retained earnings are exhausted, the issuance of new common stock imposes a higher cost of common equity and, accordingly, changes the WACC.

The general approach for establishing a WACC schedule is shown in Figure 4.2. The first step is to determine the points in the capital budget at which one of the component costs will change – the *break points*. One break point is the point at which future anticipated retained earnings are exhausted. Another is the point at which preferred stock flotation cost increases. Whenever there is a change in one of the component costs, there will be a break point in the WACC schedule.

FIGURE 4.2

Constructing a WACC Schedule

- *Determine the break points.*
  Whenever a component cost changes, the weighted average also changes. The *break point* is the amount of the total capital budget at which one of the component costs changes.

- *Determine WACC in intervals implied by the break points.*
  The WACC will be constant over intervals of the total capital budget for which all component costs are stable. WACC should be computed for each interval between the break points.

The second step in computing the WACC schedule is to *determine the weighted average cost of capital in the intervals that are implied by the break points.* Since the break points are the points in the total budget at which one of the component costs changes, the intervals between the break points represent ranges of the total budget over which the component costs are constant. The important information for the break points for Bishop Manufacturing is shown in Figure 4.3.

When Component Costs Change

Bishop Manufacturing can initially raise debt funds at the rate of 7.2 percent. This 7.2 percent corresponds to the yield to maturity of the company's bonds as established in Chapter 3 (Figure 3.9). This 7.2 percent rate is available, however, only for the first $5.3 million in new bonds issued. Bonds in excess of $5.3 million will require an additional 70 basis points, or 7.9 percent.[1]

---

[1] A basis point is one hundredth of 1 percent. That is, 100 basis points equal one percentage point.

In terms of preferred stock, Bishop may issue new preferred stock at a flotation cost of 4 percent. Notice that the information contained in Figure 4.3 with respect to preferred stock corresponds to the information in Chapter 3, Figure 3.12. Each share sells for $20 and next year's dividend is expected to be $2 per share. Since 2 million preferred shares are outstand-

---

FIGURE 4.3

Bishop Manufacturing Co., Component Costs of Capital

Debt

New debt funds:	k_D
≤ $5.3 million	7.2%
> $5.3 million	7.9%

Preferred stock
- P_o = $20
- D_1 = $2

New preferred stock:	F
≤ $2.3 million	4.0%
> $2.3 million	6.0%

Common equity
- P_o = $20.25
- D_1 = $1.62
- g = 0.07
- Projected net income next year = $41 million
- Projected net income available to common stock holders next year = $37 million
- Projected retention ratio = 0.25

New common stock:	F
≤ $5.57 million	10.0%
> $5.57 million	15.0%

Note: F = flotation cost

---

ing, total preferred dividends will be $4 million. New preferred stock would require a 4 percent flotation as long as the new issuance does not exceed $2.3 million. If Bishop issues more than $2.3 million in new preferred stock, the flotation cost will increase to 6 percent.

The cost of equity will depend on whether future retained earnings are used or new common stock is issued. Figure 4.3 shows that Bishop Manufacturing is expected to have income next year in the amount of $41 million. This represents a 7 percent increase over the 1998 income of $38 million. That is, the growth rate, g, is 7 percent. When the $4 million in preferred stock dividends is paid to current preferred stock shareholders, the amount available to common shareholders will be $37 million. Of this $37 million available to common shareholders, 25 percent of it – or $9.25 million – is expected to be retained in the firm. This is the amount of projected retained earnings that Bishop can reasonably expect to use to finance future capital projects.

Should $9.25 million in anticipated future retained earnings be insufficient to cover the equity need in the new project financing, Bishop will issue new common stock. Currently, Bishop's common stock is selling for $20.25 per share and next year's dividend is expected to be $1.62 per share (as noted in Chapter 3, Figure 3.15). The firm's growth rate of 7 percent should continue to be a good estimate of the long-run sustainable growth of the company. For new common stock, flotation costs initially will be 10 percent. If Bishop requires more than $5.57 million in new common stock, the flotation costs will increase to 15 percent.

Break Points

Figure 4.4 shows the calculation of break points for Bishop Manufacturing. Notice that the analysis has three separate stages – debt, preferred stock, and common equity. The analysis is organized in this way because break points are attributed to each of the three components and the break points occur at different levels of capital raising.

FIGURE 4.4

Bishop Manufacturing Co., Break Points

Debt ($W_D = 0.351$)

Debt range	Cost	Break point
0 – $5.3	0.04752[1]	$15.1[2]
> $5.3	0.05214[3]	> $15.1

Preferred stock ($W_p = 0.092$)

Preferred range	Cost	Break point
0 – $2.3	0.10417[4]	$25[5]
> $2.3	0.10638[6]	> $25

Common equity ($W_E = 0.557$)

Common equity range	Cost	Break point
0 – $9.25	0.15000[7]	$16.6[8]
$9.25 – $14.82	0.15889[9]	$26.6[10]
> $14.82	0.16412[11]	> $26.6

---

[1] k_D = 0.072 (1 – 0.34) = 0.04752

[2] D = 0.351 (TB); 5.3 = 0.351 (TB); TB = 5.3/3.51 = 15.1

[3] k_D = 0.079 (1 – 0.34) = 0.05214

[4] k_p = D_1/P_o (1 – F) = 2/20 (1 – 0.04) = 2/19.20 = 0.10417

[5] P/S = 0.092 (TB); 2.3 = 0.092 (TB); TB = 2.3/0.092 = 25

[6] k_p = D_1/P_o (1 – F) = 2/20 (1 – 0.06) = 2/18.80 = 0.10638

[7] $k_{R/E}$ = $D_1/P_o + g$ = 1.62/20.25 + 0.07 = 0.08 + 0.07 = 0.15

[8] E = 0.557 (TB); 9.25 = 0.557 (TB); TB = 9.25/0.557 = 16.6

[9] $k_{C/S}$ = D_1/P_o (1 – F) + g = 1.62/20.25 (1 – 0.10) + 0.07
= 1.62/18.225 + 0.07 = 0.08889 + 0.07 = 0.15889

[10] E = 0.557 (TB); 14.82 = 0.557 (TB); TB = 14.82/0.557 = 26.6

[11] $k_{C/S}$ = D_1/P_o (1 – F) + g = 1.62/20.25 (1 – 0.15) + 0.07
= 1.62/17.2125 + 0.07 = 0.09412 + 0.07 = 0.16412

Note:
a. Dollar amounts are in millions.
b. Costs are based on the equations in Figure 4.1.

The weights of each component correspond to the market value weights calculated in Chapter 3 (Figure 3.16). The assumption is that the firm's capital structure, or mix of debt and equity, will remain the same as Bishop raises capital for new projects.

Break Point for Debt

Considering *debt* first, note that (at least, conceptually) each dollar of the capital budget will be composed of $0.351 of debt. Accordingly, if $5.3 million of debt is raised, this will exactly exhaust the 7.2 percent debt funds that are available. Assuming a 34 percent tax rate, the after-tax cost of this segment of debt is 4.752 percent.

$$
\begin{aligned}
k_D\,(1 - t) &= 0.072(1 - 0.34) \\
&= 0.04752 \\
&= 4.752\%
\end{aligned}
$$

Furthermore, if exactly $5.3 million in debt is raised, that amount will represent 35.1 percent of the total budget, because *each dollar* in the total capital budget is composed of $0.351 of debt. Use of exactly $5.3 million in debt, in turn, implies a total budget of $15.1 million.

$$
\begin{aligned}
\text{Debt} &= (\text{Total budget})(0.351) \\
\frac{\text{Debt}}{0.351} &= \text{Total budget} \\
\frac{5.3\text{ million}}{0.351} &= \text{Total budget} \\
15.1\text{ million} &= \text{Total budget}
\end{aligned}
$$

In other words, in order to exactly exhaust the 7.2 percent debt (on a pre-tax basis), it is necessary for the total budget to be $15.1 million. For any total budget in excess of $15.1 million, the pre-tax cost of debt will be 7.9 percent or, on an after-tax basis, 5.214 percent.

Break Point for Preferred Stock

The break point for *preferred stock* is computed in similar fashion. The difference is the weight of preferred stock and the initial range of preferred stock over which the cost is constant. The weight of preferred stock is 9.2 percent and new preferred stock can be issued at a flotation cost of 4 percent for all new preferred stock up to and including $2.3 million. At a 4 percent flotation cost, the cost of preferred stock is 10.417 percent.

$$k_p = \frac{D_1}{P_0(1 - F)}$$

$$= \frac{2}{20(1 - 0.04)}$$

$$= \frac{2}{19.20}$$

$$= 0.10417$$

$$= 10.471\%$$

If this first segment of new preferred stock is exactly exhausted, this preferred stock will represent 9.2 percent of the total budget. This implies a break point when the total budget reaches $25 million.

$$\text{Preferred stock} = (\text{Total budget})(0.092)$$

$$\frac{\text{Preferred stock}}{0.092} = \text{Total budget}$$

$$\frac{2.3 \text{ million}}{0.092} = \text{Total budget}$$

$$25 \text{ million} = \text{Total budget}$$

For any total budget in excess of $25 million, the preferred stock component will require a flotation cost of 6 percent, resulting in a cost of preferred stock of 10.638 percent.

Break Points for Common Equity

The analysis for *common equity* is different from the analysis of bonds and preferred stock in one important aspect. The first range of common equity is not new common stock but is, instead, the projected retention of *future retained earnings*. As noted above, the projected retention of retained earnings for next year is $9.25 million. The cost of these future retained earnings is 15 percent.

$$k_{R/E} = \frac{D_1}{P_0} + g$$

$$= \frac{1.62}{20.25} + 0.07$$

$$= 0.08 + 0.07$$

$$= 0.15$$

$$= 15\%$$

This represents the dividend yield and growth rate that the current shareholders are earning. Since the amount of common equity used in any case represents 55.7 percent of the total budget, the use of $9.25 million in common equity (retained earnings) implies a total budget of $16.6 million.

$$\text{Common equity} = (\text{Total budget})(0.557)$$

$$\frac{\text{Common equity}}{0.557} = \text{Total budget}$$

$$\frac{9.25 \text{ million}}{0.557} = \text{Total budget}$$

$$16.6 \text{ million} = \text{Total budget}$$

If retained earnings of $9.25 million are insufficient to meet the equity needs for new project financing, the firm will be required to issue *new common stock*. If new common stock is issued, the flotation cost will be 10 percent for the first $5.57 million issued. With this flotation cost, the cost of common equity increases to 15.889 percent.

$$k_{C/S} = \frac{D_1}{P_0(1 - F)} + g$$

$$= \frac{1.62}{20.25(1 - 0.10)} + 0.07$$

$$= 0.08889 + 0.07$$

$$= 0.15889$$

$$= 15.889\%$$

The break point in the total budget when this segment of new common equity is exhausted is $26.6 million. This break point is the total budget that would exactly exhaust the projected retained earnings for next year and the amount of new common stock that can be raised at a flotation cost of 10 percent. Notice that the sum of retained earnings ($9.25 million) and common equity at a 10 percent flotation cost ($5.57 million) equals $14.82 million. Should the total budget for capital projects amount to $26.6 million, 55.7 percent will be common equity or $14.82 million. Thus a total budget of $26.6 million will exactly exhaust projected retained earnings and the 10 percent common equity. Any budget in excess of this total budget will necessitate issuing common equity at a 16.412 percent equity cost.

Figure 4.4 shows that there are four points in the total budget that are associated with a change in one of the component costs. The first change is at the point that the total budget reaches $15.1 million, when the cost of debt changes. The second break point is $16.6 million, when future projected retained earnings are exhausted. The third break point is $25 million, when the cost of preferred stock changes. The fourth break point is $26.6 million, when the first tier of new common equity is exhausted.

Computing WACCs

The second step in constructing the WACC schedule is to compute the WACC in the intervals or ranges of total budget that are implied by the break points. Figure 4.5 shows the ranges that are implied by the break points for Bishop Manufacturing:

- $0 to $15.1 million
- $15.1 to $16.6 million
- $16.6 to $25 million
- $25 to $26.6 million
- > $26.6 million.

FIGURE 4.5

Bishop Manufacturing Co., WACC Schedule

Total budget range	$w_D k_D (1 - t) + w_p k_p + w_E k_E$	WACC
0 – $15.1	0.351(0.04752) + 0.092(0.10417) + 0.557(0.15)	
	= 0.01668 + 0.00958 + 0.08355	0.10981
$15.1 – $16.6	0.351(0.05214) + 0.092(0.10417) + 0.557(0.15)	
	= 0.01830 + 0.00958 + 0.08355	0.11143
$16.6 – $25	0.351(0.05214) + 0.092(0.10417) + 0.557(0.15889)	
	= 0.01830 + 0.00958 + 0.08850	0.11638
$25 – $26.6	0.351(0.05214) + 0.092(0.10638) + 0.557(0.15889)	
	= 0.01830 + 0.00979 + 0.08850	0.11659
> $26.6	0.351(0.05214) + 0.092(0.10638) + 0.557(0.16412)	
	= 0.01830 + 0.00979 + 0.09141	0.11950

Note: Dollar amounts are in millions.

4

Within each of these ranges, the weighted average cost of capital is computed. In the range of $0 to $15.1 million, the cost of debt is 4.752 percent because of the cost of debt is 4.752 percent for all budgets up to $15.1 million. The cost of preferred stock is 10.417 percent in this range because 10.417 percent is the cost of preferred stock for all capital budgets up to and including $25 million. The range that is relevant here, $0 to $15.1 million, is within the range $0 to $25 million for which the 10.417 percent cost of preferred stock is relevant. For common equity in this range, the cost is 15 percent. The cost of common equity is 15 percent for all total capital budgets up to and including $16.6 million. The range being considered first, $0 to $15.1 million, is within that range. Weighting each of these component costs by their respective weights, the WACC in the total budget range of $0 to $15.1 million is 10.981 percent.

The second total budget range in Figure 4.5 is $15.1 to $16.6 million. The weighted average cost of capital is computed in the same way. In this range, the cost of debt is higher at 5.214 percent because a total budget of $15.1 million was the point at which the cost of debt increased. The cost of preferred stock is the same in this second range as it was for the first range because the 10.417 percent cost of preferred stock applies to all total budget ranges within the range $0 to $25 million. The cost of common equity is still 15 percent because 15 percent is the relevant cost of common equity for all total budgets from $0 to $16.6 million. When these component costs are multiplied by their respective weights, the result is a weighted average cost of capital of 11.143 percent.

The calculation of weighted average cost of capital in each range that follows incorporates the same logic as for the first two ranges.

Figure 4.5 explains the cost of capital for every dollar of capital that Bishop Manufacturing may anticipate raising. These WACCs represent the required return in the capital budgeting decision. Required rates of return are compared to expected rates of return, or internal rates of return (IRRs), of the projects in which Bishop may invest.

THE INVESTMENT OPPORTUNITY SCHEDULE

The investment opportunity schedule (IOS) is a ranking of possible projects in which a firm may invest. The IOS ranks the projects in order of priority, where priority is determined by each project's internal rate of return, or IRR. The IRR is the rate that causes the present value of future projects cash flows to exactly equal the initial investment. The initial investment is essentially the cost of the project.

Figure 4.6 outlines the steps to construct an investment opportunity schedule. The first step is to rank the projects by IRR. The project that is most preferable will appear at the top of the ranking and will have the

---

FIGURE 4.6

Constructing an Investment Opportunity Schedule

- **Rank the Projects by IRR.**
  Rank the projects in descending order of internal rate of return (IRR). The project at the top of the ranking is most preferable.

- **Identify the initial investments.**
  Each project has an initial investment requirement at time zero.

- **Compute cumulative initial investments.**
  The cumulative initial investment is the total amount of initial investment if a given project is accepted, assuming that all projects that have a higher ranking are also accepted.

---

highest IRR. The second step is to associate the required initial investment of each project as it appears in the ranking. The third step is to accumulate the dollars of total budget that would be spent if a particular project is accepted. The third step assumes that if a particular project is accepted, all projects that rank above it will also be accepted. That is, no project will be accepted unless all those projects that rank above it are also accepted.

Figure 4.7 shows an investment opportunity schedule for Bishop Manufacturing. Bishop has the ability to invest in up to five projects next year. The IOS thus summarizes the important information that is necessary to compare the projects' IRRs to the WACC schedule. The IRRs of the five projects in which Bishop may invest range from 9 percent to 15 percent. The projects are in the correct order as they are ranked in descending order of IRR.

The initial investment for these projects ranges from $3 million (Project D) to $10 million (Project A). If the first project is accepted, the cumulative initial investment will be the required investment for that project only, or $10 million. The second most attractive project has an expected return of 13 percent and an initial investment of $4 million. If both Project A ($10 million) and Project B ($4 million) are accepted, a total of

$14 million will be required for capital investment next year. The cumulative investment column amounts are a running total of all projects up to that point in the ranking. If all of the projects are accepted, Bishop's total capital budget for next year will be $29 million.

FIGURE 4.7

Bishop Manufacturing Co., Investment Opportunity Schedule

Project	IRR	Initial investment	Cumulative initial investment
A	0.150	$10	$10
B	0.130	4	14
C	0.120	5	19
D	0.105	3	22
E	0.090	7	29

Note: Dollar amounts are in millions.

THE OPTIMAL CAPITAL BUDGET

Figure 4.8 is a graphical depiction of both the WACC schedule (Figure 4.5) and the investment opportunity schedule (Figure 4.7). The horizontal axis measures dollars of total capital budget planned for next year. The vertical axis measures rate – either WACC (in the WACC schedule) or IRR (in the IOS). Generally, the optimal capital budget is the sum of initial investments for those projects whose IRR (expected rate of return) equals or exceeds its WACC (required rate of return).

In the case of Bishop Manufacturing, the acceptable projects are Projects A, B, and C because their IRRs all lie above the WACC schedule (see Figure 4.9).

The WACC for project C is a blend of several WACCs. Project C requires $5 million. Since it is the third project – after Projects A and B – this $5

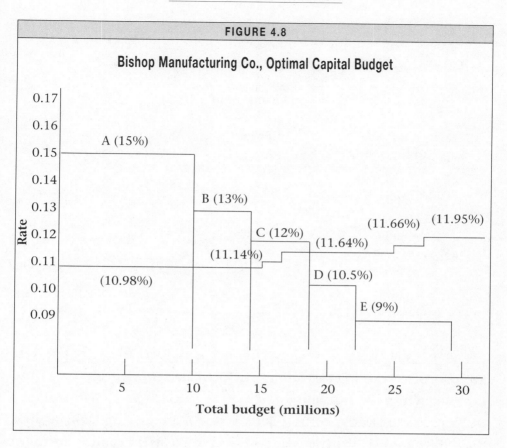

FIGURE 4.8

Bishop Manufacturing Co., Optimal Capital Budget

4

FIGURE 4.9

Bishop Manufacturing Co., Acceptable Projects

	IRR	WACC
A	15%	10.98%
B	13%	11.14%
C	12%	11.35%

million is the total budget range from $14 million to $19 million. In this range, there are three different WACCs – 10.98 percent, 11.14 percent, and 11.64 percent. The weighted average of these WACCs is 11.35 percent (see Figure 4.10).

FIGURE 4.10

Bishop Manufacturing Co., Project C, Cost of Capital

Dollars in the total budget to fund Project C	Percentage of total cost of Project C (decimal)	Applicable WACC	Weighted WACC
$14 to $15.1 million = $1.1 million	0.22	10.98%	2.42
$15.1 to 16.6 million = $1.5 million	0.30	11.14%	3.34
$16.6 to $19 million = $2.4 million	0.48	11.64%	5.59
Total	1.00	n/a	11.35%

For Project D, the expected return is 10.5 percent but the weighted average cost of capital for that project is 11.64 percent. For Project E, the expected return is 9 percent but the WACC ranges from 11.64 percent to 11.95 percent. Clearly, both Projects D and E are unacceptable because their IRRs are below their weighted average costs of capital. In other words, their expected returns are less than their required returns.

Since Projects A, B, and C are acceptable, however, this suggests that next year's total capital budget for Bishop Manufacturing should be $19 million. This is Bishop's *optimal capital budget* which will maximize the value of projects accepted and will maximize increases in shareholder wealth associated with these projects.

A DYNAMIC PROCESS

Analyzing the cost of capital can be a dynamic process. To the extent that each component of capital can be raised at a cost that does not change, the weighted average cost of capital will not change. However, when a component cost changes, the average also will change. This circumstance necessitates construction of the WACC schedule. The WACC schedule is then compared with the firm's investment opportunity schedule, or IOS. A project will be acceptable if its IRR (as included in the IOS) coincides with or lies above the WACC schedule. The combined initial investments of the projects that meet these conditions form the firm's optimal capital budget.

4

RISK, CAPITAL PROJECTS, AND PORTFOLIO THEORY

INTRODUCTION

In the field of finance, *risk* is generally thought of as *uncertainty* that an asset will earn an expected rate of return or that a *loss* will occur. When firms invest in capital projects, risk is associated with the uncertainty of future cash flows. Capital projects are long-term and the projected cash flows are necessarily assumptions about future events. To the extent that future cash flows are highly variable, more risk is associated with the project. The likelihood of greater variability of return is an issue that may be addressed in several ways:

- incorporating a variety of possible cash flows and holding the cost of capital constant;
- adjusting risky cash flows to amounts that would be acceptable if there were no uncertainty and then using the risk-free rate as the cost of capital;
- evaluating alternative times to conclude a project while holding the cost of capital constant;
- considering a new project as part of a portfolio of projects within the firm and assessing the impact of the project on the variability of the portfolio of existing projects. This approach assesses the contribution to risk made by the new project, with higher risk justifying a higher cost of capital;
- adjusting the cost of capital for the contribution to risk associated with the new project – this approach extends portfolio theory to derive a more refined measure of risk and arrive at an appropriate cost of capital.

EXPECTED NET PRESENT VALUE

In most cases, single point estimates of future cash flows are difficult, if not impossible, to generate. It is often more feasible to generate several estimates of cash flow for a particular period, based on expectations of economic circumstances or specific events. The *expected net present value approach* incorporates the subjective probabilities of the decision maker.[1] The *probability distributions* of cash flow streams for each of the relevant years in the useful life of a project are developed.

Joint Probabilities

In some cases, the level of cash flow in later years will depend on the level of cash flow in earlier years. When the decision maker has reason to believe that this connection exists, it is necessary to use simple probabilities to arrive at *joint probabilities*. A joint probability of a specific event is the probability of the event occurring, given the probabilities of the events that precede it. Mathematically, a joint probability is the product of (1) the simple probability of occurrence and (2) the probabilities of the preceding events.

$$\text{Joint } p = \prod_{t=1}^{n} p_t$$

where Joint p = probability of occurrence in period n given the probabilities of occurrence in periods 1 through $n - 1$.

p_t = probability of occurrence in period t.

Figure 5.1 illustrates a project with a two-year estimated useful life, Project A. The initial investment for Project A is $100. In year 1, Project A could return either $100 or $50, with 0.4 and 0.6 probabilities, respectively. If the cash flow in year 1 is $100, then the cash flow in year 2 will either be $105 or $90. More specifically, if period 1 cash flow equals $100, there is a 0.3 probability of a $105 cash flow in period 2 and a 0.7 probability of a $90 cash flow in period 2. Likewise, if cash flow in year 1 is $50, the cash flow in year 2 will either be $65 with a 0.2 probability, or $40, with a 0.8 probability.

---

[1] See Appendix A, *The Mathematics of Uncertainty*.

FIGURE 5.1

Joint Probabilities, Project A

0		1		2		Joint
p	CF	p	CF	p	CF	p
1.0	<100>	0.4	100	0.3	105	0.12
				0.7	90	0.28
		0.6	50	0.2	65	0.12
				0.8	40	0.48

$$\text{Joint } p = \prod_{t=1}^{n} p_t$$

where Joint p = probability of occurrence in period n given the probabilities of occurrence in periods 1 through $n - 1$.

p_t = probability of occurrence in period t

5

The simple probability of a \$105 cash flow in year 2 is 0.3. However, this outcome depends on having realized a \$100 cash flow in period 1. Thus the joint probability of a \$105 cash flow in year 2 is 0.12 (0.4 × 0.3). Likewise, the joint probability of achieving both a \$100 cash flow in year 1 and a \$90 cash flow in year 2 is 0.28 (0.4 × 0.7).

If the cash flow in year 1 is \$50, the joint probability of a \$50 cash flow in year 1 and a \$65 cash flow in year 2 is 0.12 (0.6 × 0.2). The joint probability of a \$50 cash flow in period 1 and a \$40 cash flow in period 2 is 0.48 (0.6 × 0.8). Notice that the joint probabilities in each time period will sum to 1 as should the probabilities in each individual time period.[2]

---

[2] Note also that the probability of a \$100 outflow in period 0 is 1.0. Thus, the joint probability of an outflow of \$100 in period 0 and an inflow of \$100 in period 1 is the product of 1.0 and 0.4, or 0.4.

FIGURE 5.2

Expected Cash Flows and Present Values, Project A

$$E(CF_t) = \sum_{s=1}^{n} p_s \, CF_{st}$$

where $E(CF_t)$ = expected cash flow at time t

s = state of nature

n = total number of states of nature

p_s = probability of state of nature s

CF_{st} = cash flow at time t in state of nature s

$E(CF_1)$ = 0.4(100) + 0.6(50)

= 40 + 30

= $\underline{\underline{70}}$

$E(CF_2)$ = 0.12(105) + 0.28(90) + 0.12(65) + 0.48(40)

= 12.60 + 25.20 + 7.80 + 19.20

= $\underline{\underline{64.80}}$

$E(NPV_A)$ = 70/(1.10) + 64.8/(1.10)² − 100

= 63.64 + 53.55 − 100

= 117.19 − 100

= $\underline{\underline{17.19}}$

Computing Expected Net Present Value

Figure 5.2 extends expectation theory to cash flows associated with capital projects. Notice that the expectation of a given cash flow, $E(CF_t)$, is the sum of all products of (1) the probability of a cash flow in a given state of nature and (2) the cash flow itself.

$$E(CF_t) = \sum_{s=1}^{n} p_s \, CF_{st}$$

where $E(CF_t)$ = expected cash flow at time t

s = state of nature

n = total number of states of nature

p_s = probability of state of nature s

CF_{st} = cash flow at time t in state of nature s

Using the probability distribution in Figure 5.1, the expected cash flow for period 1 is $70. This is computed by multiplying the probability of 0.4 by the cash flow of $100 and then adding to this result the product of (1) the probability of 0.6 and (2) the cash flow of $50.

In the case of year 2, the joint probabilities are each multiplied by their respective cash flows and then these products summed to arrive at an expected cash flow in year 2 of $64.80. When these expected cash flows are discounted at the cost of capital of 10 percent (given in this case) and the $100 initial investment subtracted, the expected net present value of Project A is $17.19.

$$E(NPV_A) = \sum_{t=1}^{n} \frac{E(CF_t)}{(1 + k)^t} - I$$

where $E(NPV_A)$ = expected net present value of project A

$\quad E(CF_t)$ = expected cash flow at time t

$\qquad\quad k$ = cost of capital

$\qquad\quad n$ = number of years of expected life of project

$\qquad\quad I$ = initial investment.

It should be noted that in cases of uncertain cash flows, it is possible that subsequent-year cash flows will not necessarily be contingent on previous-year cash flows. That is, cash flows in each subsequent year may be independent of cash flows in previous years. In such cases, the expected cash flow for a specific year is simply the product of probabilities (for example, year 1 probabilities) and associated cash flows.

CERTAINTY EQUIVALENTS AND RISK PREFERENCE

An alternative approach to evaluating cash flows that are not known with certainty is to convert them to *certainty equivalents*. Adopting this approach enables the decision maker to adjust the cash flows for perceived increases in risk over time.

An Intuitive Understanding of Certainty Equivalents

A certainty equivalent is a cash flow which, if received with certainty in the future, causes a decision maker to be indifferent between it and a more risky cash flow received at the same time. A certainty equivalent cash flow, CE, discounted at the risk-free rate will yield the same present value as a more risky cash flow, CF, discounted at the appropriate risk-adjusted discount rate.

For example, suppose that a decision maker is faced with the following alternatives.

- **Alternative I.** Accept a one-year project. If the project succeeds, the net cash flow will be $1 million. If the project fails, the net cash flow will be zero. The probability of success is 0.50.
- **Alternative II.** Do not accept the project and receive a risk-free $250,000.

The expected cash flow of the project is $500,000. However, if the decision maker is indifferent between the project (Alternative I) and receiving a risk-free $250,000 (Alternative II), the certainty equivalent is $250,000.[3]

Since the decision maker is indifferent between the two alternatives, both have an equivalent value. That is, the present value of the two are equal. The present values are determined using the appropriate discount rates – risk-adjusted cost of capital for the risky alternative, risk-free rate for the certainty equivalent.

---

[3] If the decision maker prefers Alternative I, the certainty equivalent is not $250,000, but some higher amount. Generally, a decision maker whose certainty equivalent is less than the expected outcome (based on probabilities) is considered risk averse. If the certainty equivalent is higher than the expected outcome, the decision maker is risk seeking. When the certainty equivalent equals the expected outcome, the individual is risk neutral.

$$\frac{CE_t}{(1 + k_{rf})^t} = \frac{E(CF_t)}{(1 + k)^t}$$

where CE_t = certainty equivalent of risky future cash flow $E(CF_t)$

k = cost of capital for risky cash flows

k_{rf} = risk-free discount rate.

The certainty equivalent approach requires that a decision maker assesses his or her own preference for risk, permitting greater adjustment for risk in latter years of the project if appropriate.

Adjusting Cash Flows to Certainty Equivalents

The certainty equivalent relationship can be used to adjust future cash flows and compute NPV. Figure 5.3 shows that the certainty equivalent, CE_t, of a given cash flow is the risky cash flow or the $E(CF_t)$, multiplied by a factor and that the factor is the ratio of $\frac{(1 + k)^t}{(1 + k_{rf})^t}$. The risk free rate is an objectively determined rate – usually the government securities rate – that is appropriate for the number of periods that elapse between the point of valuation and the cash flow itself. For example, for a cash flow that is

---

FIGURE 5.3

Certainty Equivalent

$$\frac{CE_t}{(1 + k_{rf})^t} = \frac{E(CF_t)}{(1 + k)^t}$$

$$CE_t = E(CF_t) \frac{(1 + k_{rf})^t}{(1 + k)^t}$$

where CE_t = certainty equivalent of risky future cash flow $E(CF_t)$

k = discount rate for risky cash flows

k_{rf} = risk-free discount rate

---

expected two years from time zero, the appropriate risk free rate would be the two-year government securities rate. The risk-adjusted discount rate will not necessarily be the same for every decision maker. In fact, the discount rate can be varied for each year of the relevant time period. For example, a cash flow received in two years may be discounted at one rate for the second year and at another rate for the first year. In such a case, the product of the discounting factors, $(1 + k_1)(1 + k_2)$ – instead of $(1 + k)^2$ – will reflect the decision maker's perception of increased risk over time.

Computing NPV with Certainty Equivalents

Figure 5.4 shows an example of adjusting risk-adjusted cash flows to certainty-equivalent cash flows. As noted earlier in the chapter, Project A has the following expected cash flows:

FIGURE 5.4

Certainty-Equivalent Cash Flows and Net Present Value, Project A

$$CE_1 = 70 \left[\frac{(1.05)}{(1.10)} \right]$$

$$= 66.82$$

$$CE_2 = 64.80 \left[\frac{(1.05)^2}{(1.10)(1.12)} \right]$$

$$= 57.99$$

$$NPV_{CE} = \frac{66.82}{(1.05)} + \frac{57.99}{(1.05)^2} - 100$$

$$= 63.64 + 52.60 - 100$$

$$= \underline{\underline{16.24}}$$

where NPV_{CE} = certainty equivalent NPV

$$I_0 = 100$$
$$E(CF_1) = 70$$
$$E(CF_2) = 64.80.$$

It is assumed that the government securities yield curve is flat, that is, that the rate for one-year government securities is also the rate for two-year securities.[4] It is also assumed that the yield curve for assets in this risk class is flat at 10 percent, but that there is an adjustment for the passage of time, that is, the cash flows which are received in later periods are more risky and have a higher cost of capital (two percentage points higher).

Substituting the values of cash flow and appropriate discount rates to cash flow 1, the certainty equivalent cash flow is $66.82. For year 2, the certainty equivalent is $57.99. These certainty-equivalent cash flows are then discounted at the risk free rate for the appropriate number of periods so that their present values are $63.64 and $52.60 for years 1 and 2, respectively. The certainty-equivalent net present value of Project A is $16.24. This is slightly lower than the net present value computed originally (Figure 5.2) because of the decision maker's perception of increasing riskiness over time.

The certainty-equivalent approach allows a decision maker to adjust for the level of risk associated with each cash flow over time. The most problematic aspect of this approach is that the adjustment for risk is subjective. The risk preferences of the decision maker (perhaps a professional financial manager) may not be the same as those of the shareholders of the firm. Also adjusting the cost of capital for the passage of time is subjective. Nevertheless, the concept is sound in terms of assumptions and implications of risk perception. Certainty equivalents provide flexibility in adjusting for risk in capital investment decision making.

---

[4] The rate for two-year securities is the average of the one-year rate for the first year and the one-year rate for the second year. Since the two-year average is the same as the one-year rate for year 1, the one-year rate for year 2 is the same as that for the first year.

DECISION-TREE ANALYSIS WITH A CONSTANT COST OF CAPITAL

Project A may also be evaluated using *decision-tree* analysis. A decision tree describes alternative outcomes in subsequent periods, given specific outcomes in earlier periods. Figure 5.5 illustrates how a decision tree might be constructed using the anticipated cash flows of Project A in Figure 5.1. Notice that all of the information with respect to cash flows and their associated probabilities is included in the decision tree.

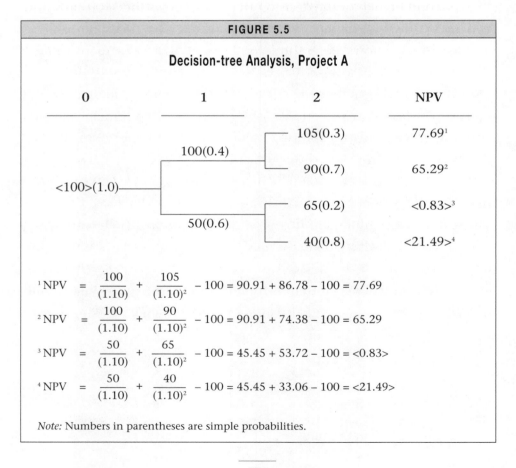

FIGURE 5.5

Decision-tree Analysis, Project A

0	1	2	NPV
		105(0.3)	77.69[1]
	100(0.4)		
		90(0.7)	65.29[2]
<100>(1.0)			
		65(0.2)	<0.83>[3]
	50(0.6)		
		40(0.8)	<21.49>[4]

[1] $NPV = \dfrac{100}{(1.10)} + \dfrac{105}{(1.10)^2} - 100 = 90.91 + 86.78 - 100 = 77.69$

[2] $NPV = \dfrac{100}{(1.10)} + \dfrac{90}{(1.10)^2} - 100 = 90.91 + 74.38 - 100 = 65.29$

[3] $NPV = \dfrac{50}{(1.10)} + \dfrac{65}{(1.10)^2} - 100 = 45.45 + 53.72 - 100 = <0.83>$

[4] $NPV = \dfrac{50}{(1.10)} + \dfrac{40}{(1.10)^2} - 100 = 45.45 + 33.06 - 100 = <21.49>$

Note: Numbers in parentheses are simple probabilities.

Determining NPV for Each Possible Combination

The primary difference in Figure 5.5 as compared to Figure 5.1 is that a net present value is associated with each "branch" of the tree. For the first branch, the $100 initial investment has a probability of 1.0. Notice that all subsequent branches emerge from this "decision node."

The first branch from time zero leads to a cash flow of $100. This cash flow has a 0.4 probability. From this node in the decision tree, year 2 cash flow may be $105 with a 0.3 probability or a $90 with a 0.7 probability.

Following the first branch, or highest branch as depicted in Figure 5.5, the initial investment is followed by a $100 cash flow in year 1 and a $105 cash flow in year 2. Using a 10 percent discount rate, the net present value for this branch of the decision tree is $77.69.

The second branch of the decision tree also follows the $100 cash flow in year 1. However, its year-2 cash flow is $90 with a 0.7 probability. Given these cash flows along the second branch, the net present value is $65.29.

Branches 3 and 4 follow the path of a $100 initial investment at period 0 and a $50 cash flow in period 1. In period 2, branch 3 includes a $65 cash flow with a 0.2 probability. The net present value of branch 3 is a −$0.83.

Branch 4 also has a $50 cash flow in year 1 but is followed by a $40 cash flow in year 2. Its net present value is a −$21.49.

By following each branch, it is possible to determine the ultimate net present value of Project A under certain assumptions. Notice that the cash flows and associated probabilities in Figure 5.5 are identical to those in Figure 5.1. The difference is that the branches of a decision tree have been constructed so that each possible combination of cash flows is now associated with a net present value.

FIGURE 5.6

Decision-tree Analysis, Expected Net Present Value, Project A

$$E(NPV_A) = 0.12(77.69) + 0.28(65.29)$$
$$- 0.12(0.83) - 0.48(21.49) - 100$$
$$= 9.3228 + 18.2812 - 0.0996 - 10.3152$$
$$= 17.1892$$
$$= \underline{17.19}$$

Computing Expected NPV

Figure 5.6 takes the decision-tree analysis one step further by finding the expected net present value, E(NPV).

$$E(NPV_A) = \sum_{s=1}^{n} jp_s NPV_{As}$$

where NPV_A = expected NPV of Project A

s = state of nature or "branch" of tree decision tree

n = total number of states of nature

jp_s = joint probability of state of nature s

NPV_{As} = NPV of Project A in state of nature s.

The expected net present value is computed as the sum of all products of (1) net present value and (2) the associated probability.

The first term on the right-hand side of the equation in Figure 5.6 is the product of the net present value of $77.69 (Branch 1) and the joint probability of occurrence of this net present value. The joint probability of the net present value of $77.69 is the probability of a $105 cash flow in year 2, given a $100 cash flow in year 1, and a $100 initial investment in period 0. The joint probability of 0.12 is computed as the product of the simple probabilities of each of those events [(1.0)(0.4)(0.3)].

Likewise, the second term on the right-hand side of the equation in Figure 5.6 is the product of the NPV of $65.29 (Branch 2) and its joint probability. In this second branch of the decision tree, the 0.28 probability of a $65.29 net present value is the probability of a $90 cash flow in year 2, given a $100 cash flow in year 1, and an initial investment of $100 in year 0 [(1.0)(0.4)(0.7)].

Each subsequent joint probability is calculated in the same way. Because the net present value in Branches 3 and 4 of the decision tree are negative, the inclusion of these two NPVs reduces the E(NPV).

When the initial investment of $100 is subtracted, the expected net present value of Project A is $17.19, the same as that obtained in Figure 5.2. The decision-tree analysis allows a decision maker to focus on the outcomes (branches of the tree) that will ultimately lead to a positive net present value, that is, an acceptable project. While the net present value calculation in Figure 5.2 is positive, it is not apparent that a $50 cash flow in year 1 will result ultimately in a negative net present value, because year-2 cash flows, given a $50 cash flow in year 1, will not be sufficiently large to ensure an acceptable project (non-negative NPV). Thus, while the expected net present value is positive in both cases, the decision-tree analysis clearly indicates the possibility of a unprofitable project.

THE ABANDONMENT DECISION WITH CONSTANT COST OF CAPITAL

When a capital project carries with it a non-zero salvage value, it may be desirable to analyze the project in terms of an abandonment date. In some cases, abandoning a project before its estimated useful life has elapsed can yield a higher NPV than continuing the project to the end of its useful life. The *abandonment decision* can be viewed in the context of both certain cash flows and uncertain cash flows.

FIGURE 5.7

Net Present Value Under Abandonment Alternative

$$NPV = \left[\sum_{t=1}^{b} \frac{CF_t}{(1+k)^t} \right] - I - \frac{SV}{(1+k)^b}$$

where b = time of abandonment

I = initial investment

SV = salvage value (net of tax)

Abandonment in the Certainty Case

The basic approach to the abandonment decision is to consider abandoning a project at each possible year in the expected useful life. For each iteration of the abandonment decision, the salvage value of the project must be estimated. The first iteration assumes abandonment after the first year, the second after the second year, and so on.

$$NPV = \left[\sum_{t=1}^{b} \frac{CF_t}{(1+k)^t} \right] - I - \frac{SV}{(1+k)^b}$$

where b = time of abandonment

I = initial investment

SV = salvage value (net of tax).

As seen in Figure 5.7, only those cash flows up to time b, time of abandonment, are included in each iteration. The initial investment is subtracted and the salvage value of the project as of time b is discounted for the appropriate number of periods using a constant cost of capital. The equation in Figure 5.7 is applied to each year for the useful life of the project. Once this has been accomplished, resulting net present values are compared. The iteration that results in the highest net present value then dictates the optimal time of abandonment.

FIGURE 5.8

Abandonment Analysis, Project B

	0	1	2	3
Cost	<100>			
Cash flows		40	80	110
Salvage values		70	20	10

Net present value

For $b = 1$,

$$\text{NPV} = \frac{40}{(1.10)} - 100 + \frac{70}{(1.10)}$$

$$= 36.36 - 100 + 63.64$$

$$= \underline{\underline{0}}$$

For $b = 2$,

$$\text{NPV} = \frac{40}{(1.10)} + \frac{80}{(1.10)^2} - 100 + \frac{20}{(1.10)^2}$$

$$= 36.36 + 66.12 - 100 + 16.53$$

$$= \underline{\underline{19.01}}$$

For $b = 3$,

$$\text{NPV} = \frac{40}{(1.10)} + \frac{80}{(1.10^2)} + \frac{110}{(1.10)^3} - 100 + \frac{10}{(1.10)^3}$$

$$= 36.36 + 66.12 + 82.64 - 100 + 7.51$$

$$= \underline{\underline{92.63}}$$

Note: All cash flows are net of tax.

Consider Figure 5.8. Project B is a three-year project with an initial investment of $100. The future cash flows are $40, $80, and $110, respectively, in the three years of useful life. According to the approaches of net present value that have been discussed thus far, the cash flows in each of these three years are discounted to their present value at time zero and the initial investment subtracted. Only the salvage value of the end of year 3 is normally considered. However, in performing an abandonment-decision analysis, net present value is calculated assuming abandonment after year 1, then year 2, and finally year 3.

Specifically, when $b = 1$, there are two cash flows in year 1 – the normal operating cash flow of $40 and the salvage value of $70. When these are discounted at the assumed 10 percent cost of capital and the initial investment of $100 is subtracted, net present value is zero.

When $b = 2$, the operational cash flows of $40 and $80 are received in periods 1 and 2, respectively. At the end of year 2, the salvage value is estimated at $20. The present value of this salvage value is added to the present value of operational cash flows and the initial investment of $100 is subtracted. In this case, the net present value of the project is $19.01.

When $b = 3$, all operational cash flows are received and discounted at the constant cost of capital for the appropriate number of periods. However, the anticipated salvage value is only $10 if the project runs its full three-year life cycle. When the present value of the positive cash flows is added and the initial investment subtracted, the net present value is $92.63.

Under these conditions, net present value is optimized when the project is allowed to run for the full three years. This is attributable to Project B's operational cash flows, which are substantially higher than its salvage value. In fact, the cash flows increase over time, while the salvage values decrease. If operational cash flows had not increased in this way, but had been estimated to be more level, earlier abandonment may have been suggested.

The cost of capital is not adjusted in this process. The abandonment decision is a matter of timing and is completely under the discretion of the decision maker.

Abandonment Under Uncertainty

The abandonment decision may also be analyzed in the context of uncertain cash flows. Using Project A (from Figures 5.1 and 5.5) as the example,

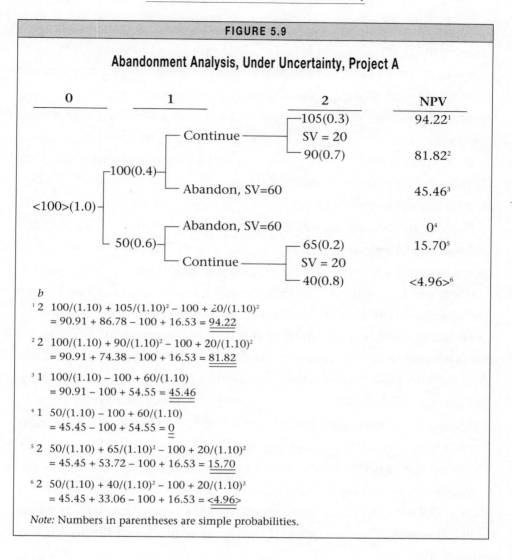

FIGURE 5.9

Abandonment Analysis, Under Uncertainty, Project A

0	1	2	NPV

Continue ——— 105(0.3) → 94.22[1]

SV = 20

90(0.7) → 81.82[2]

100(0.4)

Abandon, SV=60 → 45.46[3]

<100>(1.0)

Abandon, SV=60 → 0[4]

50(0.6)

65(0.2) → 15.70[5]

Continue ——— SV = 20

40(0.8) → <4.96>[6]

b

[1] 2 $100/(1.10) + 105/(1.10)^2 - 100 + 20/(1.10)^2$
   $= 90.91 + 86.78 - 100 + 16.53 = \underline{94.22}$

[2] 2 $100/(1.10) + 90/(1.10)^2 - 100 + 20/(1.10)^2$
   $= 90.91 + 74.38 - 100 + 16.53 = \underline{81.82}$

[3] 1 $100/(1.10) - 100 + 60/(1.10)$
   $= 90.91 - 100 + 54.55 = \underline{45.46}$

[4] 1 $50/(1.10) - 100 + 60/(1.10)$
   $= 45.45 - 100 + 54.55 = \underline{0}$

[5] 2 $50/(1.10) + 65/(1.10)^2 - 100 + 20/(1.10)^2$
   $= 45.45 + 53.72 - 100 + 16.53 = \underline{15.70}$

[6] 2 $50/(1.10) + 40/(1.10)^2 - 100 + 20/(1.10)^2$
   $= 45.45 + 33.06 - 100 + 16.53 = \underline{<4.96>}$

Note: Numbers in parentheses are simple probabilities.

assume a salvage value of $60 at the end of year 1 and a salvage value of $20 at the end of year 2.[5]

Figure 5.9 contains the same information as the decision tree in Figure 5.5. In this case, however, two additional branches have been added. It is now possible to abandon after year 1. Since there are two possible cash flows in year 1, this adds essentially two branches to the decision tree –

---

[5] Note that the earlier analyses of Project A implicitly assumed a salvage value of zero.

(1) abandonment if the cash flow in year 1 is $100 and (2) abandonment if the cash flow in year 1 is $50. The total number of branches is now 6.

The net present value of each branch is based on the cash flows that will be realized according to the relevant abandonment assumption. For example, the first branch of the decision tree assumes an initial invest-ment of $100, a cash flow of $100 in year 1, the decision to continue, an operational cash flow of $105 in year 2, and a salvage value of $20 in year 2. Using a 10 percent discount rate, the net present value of the first branch of the decision tree is $94.22.

The second branch of the decision tree also assumes a $100 initial investment in year 0 and a $100 cash flow in year 1. The decision is, again, to continue. However, the operational cash flow in year 2 is $90 (instead of $105), with the same salvage value of $20. In this case, the net present value is $81.82.

The third branch of the decision tree is a new component of this analy-sis. It assumes a $100 investment in year 0, a $100 cash flow in year 1, the decision to abandon the project at the end of year 1, and the realization of a salvage value of $60. Essentially, the project is converted from a two-year project to a one-year project with a $60 salvage value. Under these assumptions, the net present value is $45.46.

The fourth branch of a decision tree also implies only a one-year pro-ject because of abandonment at the end of year 1. The projected cash flows are a $100 initial investment in year 0, a $50 cash flow from opera-tions in year 1, the decision to abandon after receipt of the first opera-tional cash flow, and salvage value of $60. The net present value of the fourth branch of the decision tree is zero.

The fifth branch of the decision tree includes the decision to continue for the full useful life of the project. The initial investment of $100 is fol-lowed by a $50 cash flow in year 1, the decision to continue, a $65 opera-tional cash flow in year 2, and a $20 salvage value also in year 2. Net present value under these circumstances is $15.70.

The sixth branch of the decision tree involves a $100 initial investment, a $50 cash flow in year 1 from operations, a decision to continue, a $40 operational cash flow in year 2 and a $20 salvage value. The net present value of the sixth branch of the decision tree is –$4.96.

This type of analysis enables a decision maker not only to arrive at an "accept" or "reject" conclusion with respect to a capital project, but also to analyze the optimal point at which the project should be concluded. The analysis may be conducted under the assumption of certain or uncertain cash flows. In Figure 5.8, cash flows for Project B were assumed to be known with certainty and analysis of the abandonment decision led to the conclusion that the project be continued for its full useful life.

In Figure 5.9, Project A cash flows are not known with certainty. It is clear that if the cash flow in year 1 is $100, all net present values of the project will be positive whether or not it is abandoned at the end of year 1. If it is abandoned at the end of year 1, the net present value of the project is $45.46. If the project is continued after year 1, NPV will be either $94.22 (0.30 probability) or $81.82 (0.7 probability). In either case, it is clear that the project should be continued if the cash flow in year 1 is $100.

On the other hand, the decision with respect to abandonment is not as clear-cut if the cash flow in year 1 is $50. If the decision is made to abandon the project after receipt of $50 in year 1, NPV is zero. This means that the project will return exactly the 10 percent that is required by the suppliers of capital. On the other hand, if the decision is made to continue after this point there is a 0.2 probability for a $15.70 net present value and a 0.8 probability for a –$4.96 net present value. The expected net present value under these circumstances is –$0.83.[6] Thus, the appropriate decisions in the event of a $50 cash flow in year 1 is to abandon the project at that point. Doing so will exactly compensate the suppliers of capital at their required rates of return. Not to do so yields a slightly negative expected NPV and will fail to earn the cost of capital.

The abandonment decision may be analyzed in the context of either certain or uncertain cash flows. The decision-tree analysis is useful in that

5

---

[6] The expected net present value if the project is continued after $50 has been received in year 1 is the sum of the products of the two net present values and their associated probabilities of 0.2 and 0.8.

it facilitates a clear mapping of the alternatives and their associated financial outcomes.

SENSITIVITY ANALYSIS

Every aspect of capital investment will have an impact on the ultimate outcome. Even when probability distributions are established, it is often useful to test the viability of the project under other assumed probability distributions. This can be accomplished either by changing the cash flows themselves, by changing the probabilities, or by some combination of these changes. The resulting range of net present values at a constant cost of capital or internal rates of return will indicate for the decision maker just how sensitive the decision is to the level of cash flows that is assumed. Figure 5.10 shows the other factors to take into account.

FIGURE 5.10
Sensitivity Analysis
■ Cash flow
■ Estimated life
■ Discount rate

If the resulting NPVs are all significantly greater than zero, it can be concluded that the analysis is not heavily dependent on precise estimation of future cash flows. This means that the decision maker can feel greater assurance as to the accuracy of the analysis and the decision. On the other hand, if changes in cash flow assumption (within reasonable limits) cause the project to become unacceptable, then the decision maker should analyze the project more fully before making a final decision.

The abandonment-decision analysis in the section above addresses the issue of sensitivity to the estimated useful life of the project. A sensitivity analysis of estimated useful life would assume that the total years available are not necessarily those first estimated. For example, a project with a ten-year useful life should be analyzed assuming that its useful life is actually five, six, seven, eight, or nine years instead of ten. If the project's NPV quickly goes negative when a shorter estimated useful life is assumed, perhaps at eight or nine years, the decision maker is alerted that the useful life of the project is critical in making the correct decision. On the other hand, if reducing the useful life by some moderate number of years does not cause net present value to become negative, then the results can be accepted with a higher degree of confidence.

The same can be said for the cost of capital. A project may be only marginally acceptable because (1) internal rate of return equals or only slightly exceeds the cost of capital or (2) net present value is zero or only slightly higher than zero. In such a case, the decision will be sensitive to the assumed cost of capital. To test for such sensitivity, the cost of capital should be changed and the analysis repeated. Higher and lower discount rates should be selected within a relevant range. If there are substantial changes in the net present value of the project for relatively minor changes in cost of capital, this is a signal that the project should be analyzed more closely. Alternatively, if the results of the analysis are robust even in light of changes in discount rate, the decision maker can feel a greater sense of confidence in the results.

PORTFOLIO THEORY AND THE COST OF CAPITAL

Capital projects generally are considered individually when being evaluated for potential adoption. Once implemented, however, new projects coexist with existing projects and assets of the firm. Thus, there is a connection between portfolio theory (commonly associated with securities investment activities) and the cost of capital. In this sense, the assets of a firm may be viewed as a collection of assets or a portfolio of individual projects. The cost to finance this portfolio of projects will be affected by the portfolio effects within the asset pool.

Diversification of Portfolios

The benefits of *diversification* of investments are summarized in Figure 5.11. Component assets are those which form a *portfolio* of assets. The basic premise is that the expected returns of a portfolio will be linearly related to the expected returns of component assets, that is, the *expected return* of a portfolio is the weighted average of the expected returns of component assets. The weights depend on the amount that is invested in each component asset. In other words, the weights represent the relative market value of each respective asset in the portfolio.

FIGURE 5.11
Portfolio Theory
■ Portfolio expected returns are linear combinations of expected returns of component assets.
■ Portfolio variance depends on comovement of returns of component assets.

On the other hand, portfolio *variance* depends more on the way the returns of component assets move in relation to each other, or how they *covary*. In fact, if assets within a portfolio covary in a specific way, it is possible to eliminate all variability or risk within the portfolio.

Examining Two Separate Lines of Business

Figure 5.12 illustrates two lines of business and their sales for the past four years. Notice that Business A has sales that have ranged from $25 million

FIGURE 5.12		
Separate Lines of Business Sales, in Millions of Dollars		
Year	Business A Sales	Business B Sales
1	70	30
2	25	75
3	80	20
4	50	50

FIGURE 5.13

Separate Lines of Business, Expected Sales and Variability of Sales, in Millions of Dollars

Expected sales

$$k' = \frac{\left[\sum\limits_{t=1}^{N} k_t \right]}{N}$$

where k' = expected sales

N = number of observations

Business A: k_A' = (70 + 25 + 80 + 50)/4 = 225/4 = 56.25
Business B: k_B' = (30 + 75 + 20 + 50)/4 = 175/4 = 43.75

$$\sigma^2 = \frac{\left[\sum\limits_{t=1}^{N} (k_t - k')^2 \right]}{(N-1)}$$

Variability of sales

Business A: σ_A^2 = $[(70 - 56.25)^2 + (25 - 56.25)^2$
$+ (80 - 56.25)^2 + (50 - 56.25)^2]/3$
= $[189.0625 + 976.5625$
$+ 564.0625 + 39.0625]/3$
= $[1{,}768.75]/3$
= 589.5833
σ_A = 24.2813

Business B: σ_B^2 = $[(30 - 43.75)^2 + (75 - 43.75)^2$
$+ (20 - 43.75)^2 + (50 - 43.75)^2]/3$
= $[189.0625 + 976.5625$
$+ 564.0625 + 39.0625]/3$
= $[1{,}768.75]/3$
= 589.5833
σ_B = 24.2813

5

to $80 million, while Business B has sales that have ranged from $20 million to $75 million. These lines of business will be analyzed, first, in terms of their individual characteristics and, secondly, in terms of a portfolio.

Since the sales of Businesses A and B are historical data, the expected sales and variance of sales volume are computed using the approaches developed for historical data.[7] The expected return of each line of business is computed by summing all observations and dividing this sum by the number of observations (4). As shown in Figure 5.13, the expected sales level for Business A is $56.25 million. In the case of Business B, expected sales amount to $43.75 million.

The variability of sales is computed by finding the deviation of each observation from the mean, squaring each deviation, summing the squared deviations, and dividing this result by the quantity $(N - 1)$, where N is the number of observations. The variance for both Business A and Business B is almost $590 million and the standard deviation of sales is slightly more than $24 million for each. The results confirm the initial intuition that these two lines of business are quite risky. That is, sales volume is quite variable. The standard deviation of sales for Business A is almost 50 percent of the expected sales volume. In the case of Business B, the standard deviation exceeds 50 percent of the expected sales level. Thus, the risk per unit of return is quite high for each of these two lines of business.

A Portfolio of Businesses

When the businesses are considered separately, each is very risky. However, when the two businesses are combined, a completely different picture emerges. When sales are combined for the two operations, the combined level of sales is a uniform $100 per year as illustrated in Figure 5.14. Notice that the $100 total is the summation of sales across lines of business.

---

[7] See Appendix A, *The Mathematics of Uncertainty*.

FIGURE 5.14

Portfolio of Businesses,
Sales Volume

Year	Sales*
1	100
2	100
3	100
4	100

* Represents the combined sales of Businesses A and B, in millions of dollars.

It is easy to see in this simple example how two variable lines of business can be combined to form a consolidated entity that has no variability of return. Figure 5.15 uses the same methodology to compute the expected sales and the variance of sales for this new combined entity. Notice that, as one would fully expect, the expected sales level is $100. Also, because each observation is exactly equal to the expected sales level, the variance of sales is zero. This combination of businesses has a positive expected return with *absolutely no risk*.

FIGURE 5.15

Portfolio of Businesses, Expected Sales and Variability of Sales,
in Millions of Dollars

Expected sales

$$k_p' = \frac{(100 + 100 + 100 + 100)}{4}$$

$$= 100$$

where k_p' = expected sales of portfolio

Variability of sales

$$\sigma_p^2 = \frac{(100 - 100)^2 + (100 - 100)^2 + (100 - 100)^2 + (100 - 100)^2}{3}$$

$$= 0$$

$$\sigma_p = 0$$

With no risk associated with this portfolio of businesses, the cost of capital should be quite low. There is no variability in cash flows and investors are not at risk.

This example illustrates the importance of comovement of returns when assets are combined. When there is a negative correlation between assets, it is possible to achieve zero variance. That is, the portfolio has zero variance because the cash flows of the two lines of business move in opposite directions offsetting each other. Referring again to Figure 5.12, notice that from year 1 to year 2 sales decreased for Business A, while sales for Business B increased. Comparing years 2 and 3, the reverse is true – Business A sales increase while Business B sales decrease. A similar pattern is observed for years 3 and 4, in that the sales of Business A decline while the sales of Business B increase. This is an example of *perfect negative correlation*.

FIGURE 5.16

Correlation Coefficient

$r_{A,B}$	Interpretation
–1	Perfect negative correlation with the maximum possible diversification benefits
0	No correlation
+1	Perfect positive correlation with no benefits from diversification

---

Figure 5.16 identifies the range of possible values for a *correlation coefficient*. Business A and Business B demonstrate a perfect negative correlation and their correlation coefficient is –1. Frequently, the correlation coefficient is denoted as $r_{A,B}$. When two lines of business have no apparent systematic comovement of returns, $r_{A,B} = 0$, that is, their movements are not related. When two assets have a perfect positive correlation, that is, they move in the same direction in roughly the same magnitude, $r_{A,B} = +1$.

From the perspective of portfolio management, a perfect negative correlation conveys maximum diversification benefits, as illustrated in the case of Businesses A and B. While this outcome is *theoretically* possible, it is *practically* impossible. Asset returns are almost never perfectly negatively correlated. However, it is not uncommon to find assets within a given economy that have a small positive correlation. While not conferring the maximum diversification benefit, a small positive $r_{A,B}$ will generate significant diversification benefits for the investor in a portfolio of assets with this correlation. In the context of capital investment, combining capital assets that exhibit something less than perfect positive correlation will confer diversification benefits on the firm. These diversification benefits will lower the risk profile of assets and reduce the cost of capital.

5

COMPUTING PORTFOLIO PARAMETERS

The discussion above presents a generally intuitive explanation of diversification and portfolio behavior. This section explains the actual calculations that are necessary to arrive at the expected return and the variance of an *n*-asset portfolio.

FIGURE 5.17

Portfolio Expected Return and Variance

Expected return

$$k_p' = \sum_{i=1}^{N} w_i k_i'$$

where k_p' = expected portfolio return

w_i = weight of asset i in portfolio

= market value of asset i as a percentage of market value of total portfolio

k_i' = expected return of individual asset i

N = number of assets in portfolio

Variance

$$\sigma_p^2 = \sum_{i=1}^{N} w_i^2 \sigma_i^2 \, i_i + \sum_{i=1}^{N} \sum_{j=1}^{N} w_i w_j \sigma_i \sigma_j r_{i,j}$$

where σ_p^2 = portfolio variance

σ_i^2 = variance of asset i

$r_{i,j}$ = correlation coefficient between assets i and j

$i \neq j$

Portfolio Expected Return

The *expected return* of a portfolio is the weighted average of the expected returns of the component assets. Figure 5.17 shows that this relationship can be summarized as follows:

$$k_p' = \sum_{i=1}^{N} w_i k_i'$$

where k_p' = expected portfolio return

w_i = weight of asset i in portfolio

= market value of asset i as a percentage of market value of total portfolio

k_i' = expected return of individual asset i

N = number of assets in portfolio

The variable k_p' is the expected return of the portfolio. In the earlier example, this variable corresponds to the $100 expected return found in Figure 5.15. The variable k_i' is the expected return of one of the component assets within the portfolio. The total number of assets within the portfolio is designated by N. Since the expected return of the portfolio is a weighted average, it is necessary to determine the weights. In each case, the weight of a component asset is the percentage that the asset represents of the total market value of the portfolio.

When the portfolio consists of two assets, the portfolio expected return is:

$$k_p' = w_A k_A' + w_B k_B'$$

Notice that the expected return of the two-asset portfolio is a linear combination of the expected returns of assets A and B, which linear combination depends on the weights of A and B within the portfolio.

Portfolio Variance

Figure 5.17 also illustrates the computation of the variance of a portfolio. The variance depends on the variability of each individual asset about its mean and on the extent of comovement between the component assets of the portfolio. In general, the portfolio variance is:

$$\sigma_p^2 = \sum_{i=1}^{N} w_i^2 \sigma_i^2 + \sum_{i=1}^{N} \sum_{j=1}^{N} w_i w_j \sigma_i \sigma_j r_{i,j}$$

where σ_p^2 = portfolio variance

σ_i^2 = variance of asset i

$r_{i,j}$ = correlation coefficient between assets i and j

$i \neq j$

This equation demonstrates that the variance of each component asset is weighted by the square of the weight of that component asset. Each such term is called a *variance term*. In addition, there is a *covariance term* for each pair of component assets within the portfolio. A covariance term is determined by the weight of each component asset in the pair, their individual standard deviations, and the way they covary with each other.

In the case of a two-asset portfolio, the portfolio variance reduces to the following form:

$$\sigma_p^2 = w_A^2\sigma_A^2 + w_B^2\sigma_B^2 + w_Aw_B\sigma_A\sigma_Br_{A,B} + w_Bw_A\sigma_B\sigma_Ar_{B,A}$$
$$= w_A^2\sigma_A^2 + w_B^2\sigma_B^2 + 2w_Aw_B\sigma_A\sigma_Br_{A,B}$$

As shown in the equation above, there are four relevant terms in the variance of a two-asset portfolio. The first is the variance term for Asset A and the second is the variance term for Asset B. The third and fourth terms are covariance terms – A as it covaries with B and B as it covaries with A. Since the third and fourth terms are identical, the variance of a two-asset portfolio contains essentially three terms: a variance term for Asset A, a variance term for Asset B, and two identical covariance terms.

As assets are added to a portfolio, the number of variance terms increases linearly. That is, a three-asset portfolio will have three variance terms. However, the covariance terms increase much faster. For example, in a three-asset portfolio has six covariance terms because there are six possible ways in which the assets can covary:

A with B

B with A

A with C

C with A

B with C

C with B.

These six covariance terms reduce to three pairs of identical terms for the combinations of A with B, A with C, and B with C.

In a four-asset portfolio, there are, again, four variance terms but six pairs of covariance terms – A with B, A with C, A with D, B with C, B with D, and C with D. For each possible pair of assets within the portfolio, two covariance terms measure the effect that was illustrated in the two lines of business noted above (see Figure 5.12).

FIGURE 5.18

Correlation Coefficient Calculation

$$r_{i,j} = \frac{\text{cov}(k_i, k_j)}{\sigma_i \sigma_j}$$

where $r_{i,j}$ = correlation coefficient between assets i and j

$\text{cov}(k_i, k_j)$ = covariance of rate of return of assets i and j

$$= \sum_{s=1}^{n} p_s (k_{is} - k_i')(k_{js} - k_j')$$

$$= \frac{\left[\sum_{t=1}^{N} (k_{it} - k_i')(k_{jt} - k_j') \right]}{N - 1}$$

(probability distribution, s = state of nature, n = number of assets)

(historical data, t = time period, N = number of time periods observed)

Correlation Coefficient

Figure 5.18 describes the calculation of the *correlation coefficient*, $r_{i,j}$. The numerator of the correlation coefficient is a *covariance*. The denominator is the product of the standard deviations of the two assets for which correlation is measured.

The covariance of return for assets i and j is very similar to the variance of return for an individual asset. Covariance can be measured either using a probability distribution or historical data.[8] In the probability distribution method, the deviation of the first asset from its expected return in a given state of nature is multiplied by the deviation of the second asset from its mean in the same state of nature. The product of these differences

---

[8] Again, see Appendix A, *The Mathematics of Uncertainty*.

is multiplied (or weighted) by the probability of that state of nature. This is repeated in each state of nature and the results are summed.

The difference between the calculation of covariance and variance is that a variance calculation requires squaring the deviation of one asset from its expected return, while a covariance calculation requires multiplying that deviation of one asset from its expected return by the corresponding deviation of a second asset. (As is true for the variance calculation, the process is repeated in each state of nature and the results are summed.)

In the case of historical data, the covariance calculation involves summing the products of the deviations for each observation and dividing the total by the term $(N - 1)$. This adjustment is comparable to the adjustment for historical data when computing variance.

To arrive at the correlation coefficient, $r_{i,j}$, the covariance is divided by the product of the standard deviations of the two assets. The correlation coefficient measures the extent to which the returns of two assets move in the same direction – positive correlation – or opposite direction – negative correlation (see also Figure 5.16).

Numerical Example of a Two-asset Portfolio

A numerical example is provided in Figure 5.19. In this example, there are four possible states of nature. In each of these states of nature, the rates of return for Asset A and Asset B are specified.

Correlation Coefficient

The first step in calculation of correlation coefficient is determining, for each asset, its expected return, variance, and standard deviation. The two expected returns are similar – 7.1 percent for Asset A and 6.9 percent for Asset B. However, the variance and standard deviation calculations produce different results. In the case of Asset A, the standard deviation is approximately 1.5 percent but is a much higher 3.1 percent for Asset B.

Notice that both assets have rates of return that are expected to move in similar directions. The range of possible outcomes of Asset B, however, is wider than the range for Asset A. Asset B is expected to have returns anywhere from 2 percent to 10 percent while the possible outcomes for Asset A range from 4 percent to 9 percent. Thus, Asset B has a higher standard deviation.

FIGURE 5.19

Two-asset Portfolio, Component Assets

Probability distribution

p_s	k_A	k_B
0.10	0.04	0.03
0.20	0.06	0.02
0.40	0.07	0.08
0.30	0.09	0.10

Expected returns

$$k_A' = 0.10(0.04) + 0.20(0.06) + 0.40(0.07) + 0.30(0.09)$$
$$= 0.004 + 0.012 + 0.028 + 0.027$$
$$= 0.071$$
$$k_B' = 0.10(0.03) + 0.20(0.02) + 0.40(0.08) + 0.30(0.10)$$
$$= 0.003 + 0.004 + 0.032 + 0.03$$
$$= 0.069$$

Variance

$$\sigma_A^2 = 0.10(0.04 - 0.071)^2 + 0.20(0.06 - 0.071)^2 + 0.40(0.07 - 0.071)^2$$
$$+ 0.30(0.09 - 0.071)^2$$
$$= 0.0000961 + 0.0000242 + 0.0000004 + 0.0001083$$
$$= 0.000229$$
$$\sigma_A = 0.015133$$
$$\sigma_B^2 = 0.10(0.03 - 0.069)^2 + 0.20(0.02 - 0.069)^2 + 0.40(0.08 - 0.069)^2$$
$$+ 0.30(0.10 - 0.069)^2$$
$$= 0.0001521 + 0.0004802 + 0.0000484 + 0.0002883$$
$$= 0.000969$$
$$\sigma_B = 0.031129$$

5

With this information, it is possible to describe some of the characteristics of a portfolio of these two assets. For purposes of this example, assume that $1,000 would be invested in Asset A and $3,000 in Asset B. In this way, the weight of Asset A is 25 percent while that of Asset B is 75 percent.[9] When these weights are applied to the expected returns for Asset A and Asset B, the result is an expected return of the portfolio of 6.95 percent (see Figure 5.20).

FIGURE 5.20

Two-asset Portfolio, Expected Return

$$k_p' = 0.25(0.071) + 0.75(0.069)$$
$$= 0.01775 + 0.05175$$
$$= 0.0695$$

Note: Weights are based on the assumption that $1,000 is invested in Asset A and $3,000 in Asset B.

The next step is to measure the extent to which these two assets are correlated, that is, to compute the correlation coefficient, $r_{A,B}$. The calculation of the numerator of $r_{A,B}$ – the covariance – is illustrated in Figure 5.21. In each state of nature, notice that the deviation of Asset A from its expected return is multiplied by the deviation of Asset B from its expected return. For example, in the first state of nature, the returns of Assets A and B are 4 percent and 3 percent, respectively (see Figure 5.19). The expected return of each asset is subtracted from these returns to arrive at deviations from the mean in the first state of nature. The product of these deviations and the probability of the first state of nature (0.10) form the first term in the calculation. Since there are four states of nature, there are four such terms.

Notice that whenever the return of an asset in a particular state of nature is below the expected return, that deviation will be negative.

---

[9] The weight of Asset A is calculated as the market value of Asset A as a percentage of the market value of the entire portfolio. Since a total of $4,000 is invested, $w_A = 0.25$. Likewise, the $3,000 that is to be invested in Asset B represents 75 percent of the total, that is, $w_B = 0.75$.

FIGURE 5.21

Two-asset Portfolio, Covariance and Correlation Coefficient

Covariance

$$
\begin{aligned}
\text{cov}\,(k_A, k_B) &= 0.10(0.04 - 0.071)(0.03 - 0.069) \\
&\quad + 0.20(0.06 - 0.071)(0.02 - 0.069) \\
&\quad + 0.40(0.07 - 0.071)(0.08 - 0.069) \\
&\quad + 0.30(0.09 - 0.071)(0.10 - 0.069) \\
&= 0.0001209 + 0.0001078 - 0.0000044 + 0.0001767 \\
&= 0.000401
\end{aligned}
$$

Correlation coefficient

$$
\begin{aligned}
r_{A,B} &= 0.000401/(0.015133)(0.031129) \\
&= 0.000401/0.000471 \\
&= 0.851380
\end{aligned}
$$

When the return of the second asset is also below its expected return, that term will also be negative. But the product of the two terms will be positive. The product of the two terms will be negative only when one of the assets is above its expected return and the other is below its expected return (in the same state of nature). Furthermore, in order for two assets to have a perfect negative correlation, one must have a return above its means whenever the other has a return below its mean.

In three of the four cases for Assets A and B (Figure 5.21), the product of their deviations is positive. This means that the two assets generally tend to move together. This is consistent with the intuitive observation that their returns seem to move in a similar fashion. When all terms (weighted by the probabilities) are summed, the covariance of the two assets is found to be 0.000401.

The correlation coefficient is this covariance divided by the standard deviations of the two assets for which the correlation is measured. In this case, the correlation coefficient is 0.851380. This means that these two assets are positively correlated, but not perfectly positively correlated. As a result, combining these two assets in a portfolio will generate diversification benefits.

FIGURE 5.22

Two-asset Portfolio, Variance

$$\sigma_p^2 = w_A^2\sigma_A^2 + w_B^2\sigma_B^2 + 2w_Aw_B\sigma_A\sigma_Br_{A,B}$$
$$= (0.25)^2(0.000229) + (0.75)^2(0.000969)$$
$$+ 2(0.25)(0.75)(0.015133)(0.031129)(0.851380)$$
$$= 0.0000143 + 0.0005451 + 0.0001504$$
$$= 0.0007098$$

$$\sigma_p = 0.0266421$$

Portfolio Variance and Standard Deviation

The variance and standard deviation of the portfolio are calculated in Figure 5.22. As noted earlier, portfolio variance depends on individual weights, standard deviations, variances, and the correlation coefficient. The variance of this portfolio is 0.0007098, while the standard deviation is 2.66 percent.

Notice that the expected return and the standard deviation of the portfolio are between the expected returns and the standard deviations of the two underlying assets (see Figure 5.23).

FIGURE 5.23

Expected Returns, Variances, and Standard Deviations

	Asset A	Asset B	Portfolio
Expected return	7.1%	6.9%	6.95%
Variance	0.0229%	0.0969%	0.0710%
Standard deviation	1.5133%	3.1129%	2.6642%

The expected return of the portfolio has an exact linear relationship to the expected returns of the underlying assets, where relative market values determine the exact nature of the linear combination. On the other hand, the standard deviation of return of the portfolio is *not* a linear combination of the standard deviations of the underlying assets.

FIGURE 5.24

Two-asset Portfolio, Weighted Average of Standard Deviations

$$
\begin{aligned}
\text{Weighted average} &= w_A\sigma_A + w_B\sigma_B \\
&= 0.25(0.015133) + 0.75(0.031129) \\
&= 0.003783 + 0.023347 \\
&= 0.027130
\end{aligned}
$$

Now consider Figure 5.24 in which the weighted average of the standard deviations of the two component assets is calculated. The weighted average is 2.71 percent, a result that is slightly larger than the actual standard deviation of the portfolio (2.66 percent). The actual portfolio standard deviation is smaller because the correlation between Assets A and B is not perfectly positive. The diversification benefits that have been derived by combining these two assets are reflected in a portfolio standard deviation that is lower than the simple weighted average of the standard deviations of the component assets.

It is this potential diversification benefit that should be considered when combining capital assets within the firm. This concept is as legitimate for fixed assets as it is for investment securities. To the extent that diversification benefits are realized, the cost of capital will be reduced.

CAPITAL ASSET PRICING MODEL: A MODEL FOR COST OF CAPITAL

One of the most important concepts in portfolio theory is the Capital Asset Pricing Model (CAPM). This theory improves on the application of portfolio principles discussed in the sections above because CAPM eliminates the necessity of computing the correlation between each pair of assets within a portfolio. Securities portfolios typically contain from 20 to 50 different assets, causing the determination of the most efficient portfolio (greatest expected return, lowest portfolio variance) to become very tedious, very quickly. CAPM avoids the necessity of computing the correlation of each pair of assets by suggesting that the critical measure of comovement is the way an asset correlates with the rest of the market. Thus, for each component asset, there is only one covariance measure that is necessary – the covariance with the market portfolio.

As shown in Figure 5.25, the improved covariance measure is beta, β. According to CAPM, the required return for a particular asset can be measured as a function of how the asset covaries with the market as a whole. The components of a required return of a particular asset are (1)

FIGURE 5.25

Capital Asset Pricing Model, Security Market Line

$$k_i = k_{RF} + \beta_i(k_m - k_{RF})$$

$$
\begin{aligned}
\text{where} \quad k_i &= \text{required return for asset } i \\
k_{RF} &= \text{risk-free rate} \\
k_m &= \text{rate of return on the market portfolio} \\
\beta_i &= \text{beta of asset } i \\
&= \frac{\text{cov}(k_i, k_m)}{\sigma_m^2} \\
k_m - k_{rf} &= \text{risk premium of the market} \\
\beta_i(k_m - k_{RF}) &= \text{risk premium of asset } i
\end{aligned}
$$

---

the risk free rate – which all assets must return – and (2) a risk premium – which is dependent on the particular asset.

Risk-free Rate

The *risk-free rate* is easily proxied as the government securities rate. A proxy for the risk-free rate is easy to obtain because of the frequent and widespread publication of prices and yields of government securities. The risk premium for the market is the difference between the market return and the risk-free rate. The market return is also relatively easy to approximate because of the number of broad-based stock indices that are frequently quoted. A broad-based index is used as a proxy for the market and its rate of return is a proxy for the market return.

Risk Premium

According to CAPM, the *risk premium* for a specific asset is the product of (1) the beta of that asset and (2) the market risk premium, where the market risk premium is the difference between the market return and the risk-free rate. An asset is considered an average asset when it has a beta of 1, that is, when it behaves as does the market. The numerator of β is the covariance of an asset return with the market return; the denominator is the variance of the market return. If an asset had exactly the same expected return as the market proxy and moved in the same ways, its covariance with the market would equal the variance of the market.[10] Since β is the ratio of (1) the covariance of a particular asset's return with the market and (2) the market variance, the "average" asset will have a beta of 1.[11]

---

[10] If Asset i behaved in exactly the same manner as the market, k_m could be substituted in every case for k_i:

$$\text{cov}(k_i, k_m) = \text{cov}(k_m, k_m) = \sigma_m^2$$

[11] If $\text{cov}(k_i, k_m) = \sigma_m^2$, $\beta_i = 1$:

$$\beta_i = \frac{\text{cov}(k_i, k_m)}{\sigma_m^2} = \frac{\sigma_m^2}{\sigma_m^2} = 1$$

Assets which are more volatile than the market have a beta that is greater than 1, while assets which are less volatile than the market have a beta that is less than 1. Unlike the range of values for the correlation coefficient, β is not limited to values between –1 to +1. Beta can have any value and theoretically can even be negative, although negative betas are extremely rare. The typical range of β is between 0.5 and 3.0. Thus, the risk premium of an asset will be some multiple of the market risk premium, where the multiple is that asset's β.

The required return for a particular asset is the sum of (1) the risk free rate and (2) the asset's risk premium. CAPM quantifies the relationship between risk and return, establishing a higher required return for assets or projects with higher volatility or risk.

Numerical Example of CAPM

The application of CAPM is illustrated in Figure 5.26. The hypothetical Project A has an internal rate of return, or expected return, of 11 percent. Using historical data, the beta of this project has been calculated as 1.5. This means that Project A (or the stock of companies in the same line of

FIGURE 5.26

Application of Capital Asset Pricing Model to Project A

Internal rate of return	0.11
Beta of Project A	1.5
Market return	0.08
Risk-free rate	0.03
Required return for Project A:	

$$k_{RF} + \beta_A(k_m - k_{RF})$$
$$= 0.03 + 1.5(0.08 - 0.03) \qquad\qquad 0.105$$

Conclusion

Accept Project A because its expected return (11 percent) exceeds its required return (10.5 percent).

business as Project A) is 1.5 times as volatile as the market as a whole. In this example, the market return and risk free rate are 8 percent and 3 percent, respectively.

Applying CAPM, the cost of capital for this project is 10.5 percent. That is, the risk of Project A (or of companies with projects similar to Project A) establishes a minimum required rate of return for the project of 10.5 percent.

From this point, the decision-making process follows the same sequence as earlier examples. Whenever the expected return (IRR) exceeds the required return, a project should be accepted. In this case, the expected return of 11 percent is 50 basis points above the required return of 10.5 percent. Thus, Project A should be accepted.

The use of the Capital Asset Pricing Model in capital budgeting decisions necessarily means that there must be a proxy for the project under consideration. There must be sufficient, comparable historical data about this proxy to measure its correlation with the market proxy. One way to obtain this data is to examine the stock returns of a firm that is primarily engaged in the same line of business as the project in question. For example, for a proposed project involving a new line of high-technology products, a good proxy may be a firm that already is engaged primarily in high-tech products. Clearly, the results will be only as reliable as the selected proxies. Accordingly, a decision maker must exercise judgment in choosing proxies for the project and for the market as a whole.

As long as the issues of proxy selection are understood, the idea of required return that is somehow based on relative volatility has useful applications. However, because the volatility of historical data does not capture the less quantifiable concepts of future market opportunity, CAPM should not be used in isolation and is best applied in the context of other techniques to establish the cost of capital.

5

MANAGING RISK IN CAPITAL PROJECTS: A SUMMARY

While cash flows cannot always be known with certainty, it is possible to incorporate the basic concepts of risk to manage the capital investment process.

- It is possible to use expected cash flows to arrive at net present value. Expected cash flow are a function of subjective probability distributions for cash flows in future years. It is even possible to incorporate conditional probabilities into the distribution of future cash flows. In these cases, the cost of capital is held constant.

- Risky future cash flows can be converted to amounts that are equivalent to the risky cash flows in a world of certainty. This involves determining the certainty equivalents of future cash flows. Certainty-equivalent cash flow will always be less than the risky cash flow. The extent to which the certainty equivalent is less than the risky cash flow will depend on the decision maker's perception of risk and the increase in risk over time. Certainty-equivalent cash flows should be discounted using the risk-free rate as the cost of capital.

- A decision-tree analysis is an organizational tool that helps to illustrate the ultimate outcome for various scenarios in the future. The decision tree incorporates the idea of joint probabilities and enables a decision maker to calculate a net present value for each possible combination of outcomes. The expected net present value can also be calculated by weighting each NPV by its appropriate joint probability of occurrence. Generally, the cost of capital is held constant.

- The abandonment decision involves analyzing a capital project in terms of whether it should be continued for its entire useful life or whether it should be abandoned prior to the end of useful life. The analysis involves assuming that abandonment will occur after each of the years of useful life and calculating NPV for each of these assumed abandonment periods. The abandonment decision can be analyzed under the assumption of certain or uncertain cash flows. The cost of capital is generally held constant.

■ All of these techniques illustrate the sensitivity of a particular decision to the assumptions on which it is based. A formal sensitivity analysis will change cash flows, estimated useful life, and the cost of capital in a number of scenarios to test the extent to which the acceptability of the project is sensitive to these factors.

■ The application of portfolio theory to the capital budgeting process adds a useful dimension to the way projects are considered. While the theories are borrowed from securities management, the concepts are, nevertheless, useful in capital investment. The basic idea is that the returns of a group of assets will be linearly related to each other and that portfolio returns will be a linear combination of the returns of the underlying (or component) assets. However, through effective diversification, it is possible to eliminate some of the variability of returns (risk) that might otherwise be encountered. In fact, if it were possible to identify two lines of business that were perfectly negatively correlated, it would be possible to eliminate all risk within the consolidated firm. While this ideal situation is virtually impossible, lesser diversification benefits may be obtained whenever the two lines of business are not perfectly positively correlated. This less-than-perfect correlation will reduce the cost of capital to the extent that diversification benefits are realized.

■ A further enhancement of the idea of diversification is the Capital Asset Pricing Model, in which the only relevant measure of comovement is the extent to which an asset covaries with the rest of the market. With this information, the cost of capital can be adjusted to more precisely compensate for the risk inherent in capital investment.

5

THE MATHEMATICS OF UNCERTAINTY

INTRODUCTION

It is often difficult to make single point estimates of cash flows when evaluating capital projects and establishing a cost of capital. In some cases, cash flows are estimated as a series of possible cash flows with a probability of occurrence associated with each. These probabilities may be used to develop an average estimated cash flow. In other cases, historical data is used to approximate future cash flows.

In using either probability distributions or historical data, variability of cash flows is also an important element in assessing risk. Uncertainty generally increases the cost of capital.

The two most important concepts in managing uncertainty are:

- expected return
- variance.

EXPECTED RATE OF RETURN

Figure A.1 shows a hypothetical Asset A that has a number of possible dollar returns. Assume that $100 is invested in Asset A at the beginning of

FIGURE A.1		
Uncertain Cash Flows, Probability Distribution, Asset A		
Probability	**Dollar return**[1]	**Rate of return**[2]
0.10	101	0.01
0.05	103	0.03
0.20	105	0.05
0.55	107	0.07
0.10	110	0.10

[1] Assuming a $100 initial investment for a period of 1 year.

[2] Represents: $\dfrac{\text{Dollar return} - \$100}{\$100}$

the period. At the end of a year Asset A can grow to at least $101 and as much as $110. The probability of each of the values is subjectively determined by the decision maker. In this case, there is a 10 percent probability that the asset will be worth $101, a 5 percent probability that it will be worth $103, a 20 percent probability that the value will be $105, and so on. Each of these outcomes is associated with a particular *state of nature* and p_s is the probability of that state of nature.

Notice that the sum of the probabilities is 1. This means that every state of nature, that is, every possible outcome, has been included in the probability distribution according to the subjective perceptions of the decision maker. Also assuming that $100 is invested in Asset A at the beginning of the period, the *dollar* returns that are noted in Figure A.1 suggest certain *rates* of return, ranging from 1 percent to 10 percent. These rates of return may also be associated with the probabilities indicated in Figure A.1.

Probability Distribution

The *probability distribution* that is shown in Figure A.1 can be used to determine the *expected return* of Asset A. An expected return is a measure of central tendency of the returns of an asset, that is, it measures the

---

FIGURE A.2

Expected Rate of Return

$$k_a' = \sum_{s=1}^{n} p_s\, k_{as}$$

where k_a' = expected rate of return of Asset A

s = state of nature

n = total number of states of nature

p_s = probability of state of nature s

k_{as} = rate of return of Asset A in state of nature s

---

approximate center of the range of values. The expected return of any probability distribution may be determined by application of the equation shown in Figure A.2. Notice that the expected return, k_a', is the weighted average of those rates of return that the decision maker anticipates, where the weight is the probability of each of the respective rates of return. In other words, the expected return is the weighted average return over all states of nature with the probability of each state of nature acting as the respective weight.[1]

FIGURE A.3

Expected Rate of Return, Asset A

$$k_a' = \sum_{s=1}^{n} p_s\, k_{as}$$

$= \ 0.10(0.01) + 0.05(0.03) + 0.20(0.05) + 0.55(0.07) + 0.10(0.10)$
$= \ 0.001 + 0.0015 + 0.01 + 0.0385 + 0.01$
$= \ \underline{\underline{0.0610}}$

Figure A.3 shows the expected return of Asset A given the probability distribution in Figure A.1. To arrive at the expected return in this case the probability of the first state of nature (0.10) is multiplied by the return of Asset A in the first state of nature (0.01). To this product is added the product of the probability of each successive state of nature and its respective rate of return. The sum of all such terms is 6.1 percent, as also shown in Figure A.3. It should be noted once again that the process of determining the expected return is a function of future estimates of outcomes. The future estimates, in turn, depend on the decision maker's belief about future outcomes and their likelihoods.

---

[1] It should be noted that expectations theory can be applied to dollar returns as well as rates of return.

Using Financial Calculators with Probability Distributions

Many models of hand-held calculators have built-in functions to compute expected return assuming a predetermined probability distribution. Figure A.4 is an example of such a calculation based on the example in Figure A.1. The first step is to clear the statistical registers of the calculator. Then the rates of return in each state of nature are input along with their probability weightings. Notice that the weights are input in Figure A.4 as whole numbers that sum to 100. Alternatively, the probabilities may be input as decimals that sum to 1. In either case, it is important to remember that the weights must be input consistently to assure reliable results.

FIGURE A.4

Expected Rate of Return, Asset A, Financial Calculator Application

Keystroke		Display
f	Σ	[To clear statistical registers.]
0.01	Enter	0.010000
10	Σ+	1.000000
0.03	Enter	0.030000
5	Σ+	2.000000
0.05	Enter	0.050000
20	Σ+	3.000000
0.07	Enter	0.070000
55	Σ+	4.000000
0.10	Enter	0.100000
10	Σ+	5.000000
	g xw	0.061000

Note: This example illustrates the use of a Hewlett-Packard 12C. Other calculators will require slightly different steps depending on the model.

After all rates of return and probabilities have been entered, the next calculator keystrokes request the weighted average by pressing the appropriate function key. The example in Figure A.4 is for the use of a Hewlett-Packard 12C. Other calculators will provide the same sort of function with perhaps slightly different keystrokes.

FIGURE A.5

Alternative Probability Distribution, Asset A

Probability	Dollar return[1]	Rate of return
0.20	101	0.01
0.45	103	0.03
0.15	105	0.05
0.10	107	0.07
0.10	110	0.10

[1] Assuming a $100 initial investment for a period of 1 year.

An Alternative Probability Distribution

Figure A.5 shows the same dollar return and rate of return distribution as that of Figure A.1. In this case, however, the decision maker has different beliefs concerning the likelihood of each one of these outcomes. The lower rates of return have been given higher probabilities. That is, the probability of a 1 percent return is now 20 percent instead of 10 percent. The probability of a 3 percent return has been increased from 5 percent to 45 percent. The probabilities of the remaining outcomes have been calculated accordingly.

The calculation of the expected rate of return under the alternative probability distribution (see Figure A6) is essentially the same. The difference is the weightings of the rates of return, that is, the probabilities of occurrence. With these probabilities, the higher weightings of lower rates of return result in a lower expected rate of return – 4 percent instead of

---

FIGURE A.6

Expected Rate of Return, Alternative Probability Distribution, Asset A

$$k_a' = \sum_{s=1}^{n} p_s \, k_{as}$$

= 0.20(0.01) + 0.45(0.03) + 0.15(0.05) + 0.10(0.07) + 0.10(0.10)

= 0.002 + 0.0135 + 0.0075 + 0.007 + 0.01

= 0.04

6.1 percent. The lower result is directly attributable to the less optimistic perceptions of this decision maker.

This example helps to illustrate the sensitivity of the expectation of rates of return to perceptions of the decision maker. While the mathematics of expected return are straightforward and unambiguously accurate, the results will always depend upon the *ex ante* belief of the decision maker or investor.

Using Historical Data

The use of a probability distribution depends on the assessment of future events by the investor or decision maker. The subjectivity of this process frequently leads investors to use past historical performance of an asset to estimate the future outcome. The objective is, nevertheless, to estimate future outcomes. In the absence of a fairly reliable probability distribution and outcomes in the respective states of nature, *historical data* may provide a good estimate of future performance. If it can be reasonably asserted that past performance is indicative of future performance, this approach is valid.

In the case of Asset A, Figure A.7 illustrates a range of historical returns. Notice that the data began with 1998, the most recent occurrence. In that year, the value of Asset A was 100. This corresponds with the previous

FIGURE A.7			
Historical Data, Asset A			
Observation	**Year**	**Value**	**Rate of return***
1	1998	100	0.0204
2	1997	98	–0.0297
3	1996	101	0.0632
4	1995	95	0.0106
5	1994	94	0.0330
6	1993	91	0.0706
7	1992	85	–0.0341
8	1991	88	0.0732
9	1990	82	0.1081
10	1989	74	0.0423
11	1988	71	0.0143
12	1987	70	–0.0278
13	1986	72	0.1613
14	1985	62	0.0690
15	1984	58	0.1837
16	1983	49	0.0426
17	1982	47	0.0682
18	1981	44	0.0476
19	1980	42	0.2000
20	1979	35	0.0938
	1978	32	———
			1.2103

* Represents: $\dfrac{\text{Current value}}{\text{Previous value}} - 1$

probability distribution in which 100 was assumed to be the value of Asset A at the beginning of the year. In the probability distribution given in Figure A.1, the future value of Asset A was estimated. In Figure A.7, past values of Asset A have been identified. To provide a statistically significant sample, 20 past observations are included.

For each of the 21 previous years, the value of Asset A at the end of each year is identified. The rate of return for that year is calculated as the ending value (EV) divided by the beginning value (BV) minus 1. This is equivalent to measuring the change in value and dividing it by the beginning value as follows:

$$\frac{(EV - BV)}{BV} = \frac{EV}{BV} - 1$$

The rates of return range from –3.41 percent to +20 percent. Notice that it is necessary to use a 1978 value in order to calculate the rate of return for 1979. That is, it is necessary to use 21 past values in order to arrive at 20 rates of return. Notice also that Figure A.7 provides a sum of the rates of return for the 20 years in the sample (1979–98).

The data used in this example show considerable variability. For some periods, the rates of return were relatively modest, while the rates of return were much higher during other periods of time. Use of such data implies a belief that future returns may be equally variable.

Decision makers should be cautious about using past as a proxy for future outcomes. If there are elements or events in the past that will not be relevant in the future, use of past data may not be well-advised. Alternatively, it may be more reliable to estimate future outcomes and associated probabilities.

Figure A.8 shows the appropriate calculation of expected rate of return with historical data. This approach is equivalent to finding the simple average of the sample observations. In this case, the probabilities associ-

---

FIGURE A.8

Expected Rate of Return, Using Historical Data

$$k_a' = \frac{\left[\sum_{t=1}^{N} k_{at}\right]}{N}$$

where k_a' = expected rate of return of Asset A

N = total number of observations

k_{at} = rate of return of Asset A in period t

$$k_a' = \frac{1.2103}{20}$$

$$= 0.060515$$

---

ated with each respective observation are equal. When N represents the number of observations in the sample, then the probability of each observation is $\frac{1}{N}$.

$$k_a' = \frac{\left[\sum_{t=1}^{N} k_{at}\right]}{N}$$

$$= \frac{1}{N}\left[\sum_{t=1}^{N} k_{at}\right]$$

$$= \left[\sum_{t=1}^{N}\left(\frac{1}{N}\right) k_{at}\right]$$

Thus, when historical data is used to arrive at the expected rate of return, the probability of each observation is the same, $\frac{1}{N}$. Applying this concept to the data in Figure A.7, the expected rate of return is 0.060515.

Using Financial Calculators with Historical Data

A financial calculator may also be used to compute the expected rate of return using historical data. In the case of the Hewlett-Packard 12C, the process is essentially to enter all of the observations into statistical registers and to request the mean return based on this input, as illustrated in Figure A.9.

After the calculator's statistical registers are cleared, each observation is entered. When there are negative rates of return, the observation is entered and the sign is changed before the number is entered in the register. The number of entries will correspond to the number of observations. Once the input is complete, the request is made for the mean rate of return and, as earlier calculated, the average rate of return is 0.060515.

FIGURE A.9

Historical Data, Expected Rate of Return, Asset A, Financial Calculator Application

Keystroke		Display
f	Σ	[To clear statistical registers.]
0.0204	Σ+	1.000000
0.0297	CHS Σ+	2.000000
0.0632	Σ+	3.000000
.		
.		
.		
0.0938	Σ+	20.000000
	g xw	0.060515

Note: This example illustrates the use of a Hewlett-Packard 12C. Other calculators will require slightly different steps depending on the model.

VARIABILITY OF RETURN

The expected rate of return measures the central tendency of a probability distribution or of past historical data. A complete evaluation of a cash flow distribution will include a description of the manner in which the observations vary from the measure of central tendency – the expected return. To the extent that these observations fluctuate from the expected return, the asset is considered to be risky. The statistics that are commonly used to measure this variability are:

- variance and standard deviation
- coefficient of variation.

FIGURE A.10

Variance

Probability distribution

$$\sigma^2_a = \sum_{s=1}^{n} p_s (k_{as} - k_a')^2$$

where σ_a^2 = variance of return of Asset A

s = state of nature

n = total number of states of nature

p_s = probability of state of nature s

k_{as} = rate of return of Asset A in state of nature s

k_a' = expected rate of return of Asset A

Historical data

$$\sigma^2_a = \frac{\left[\sum_{t=1}^{N} (k_{at} - k_a')^2\right]}{N-1}$$

where N = total number of observations

k_{at} = rate of return of Asset A in period t

171

Variance and Standard Deviation

The *variance* of an asset is the average squared deviation of returns about the asset's expected return. There are two methods of calculating variance, probability distribution and historical data, and the methods correspond to the two methods of calculating expected return.

■ The **probability distribution** approach for calculating variance is illustrated in the top portion of Figure A.10, and σ_a^2 is the symbol used to describe variance. When the calculation of variance is based on a probability distribution, the first step is to find the difference between the asset's rate of return in a given state of nature and the expected rate of return. This difference is then squared and multiplied by the probability of that state of nature. The sum of all such terms is the variance of return.

The differences between the return in a particular state of nature and the expected return must be squared before multiplication by the respective probabilities. Since the expected return is the measure of central tendency, some of the values will be greater than the mean and some will be less than the mean. If these differences are simply summed, they would cancel each other and the variance would approach zero. To overcome this, the differences are squared and then multiplied (or weighted) by the probability of their respective states of nature.

■ When **historical data** are used, the differences between the observations and the expected returns are again squared. As was the assumption in calculating the expected return using historical data, the probability of each state of nature is assumed to be the same as every other state of nature. However, instead of dividing these squared deviations by the number of observations (N), the sum of the squared deviations is divided by the quantity $N - 1$.

The squared deviations are divided by $N - 1$ instead of N because the estimate of variance using historical data is based on an estimate of the expected return. The use of historical data is a sampling technique which uses a sample expected return. Statistically, the use of a sample expected return causes the loss of one degree of freedom. In other words, an estimate is being used to arrive at another estimate. As a result, the denominator is reduced by 1.

FIGURE A.11

Variance and Standard Deviation, Probability Distribution, Asset A

$$\sigma_a^2 = 0.10(0.01 - 0.061)^2 + 0.05(0.03 - 0.061)^2 +$$
$$0.20(0.05 - 0.061)^2 + 0.55(0.07 - 0.061)^2 +$$
$$0.10(0.10 - 0.061)^2$$
$$= 0.0002601 + 0.000048 +$$
$$0.000024 + 0.000045 + 0.000152$$
$$= \underline{0.0005291}$$

$$\sigma_a = (\sigma_a^2)^{1/2}$$
$$= (0.005291)^{1/2}$$
$$= \underline{0.023002}$$

When using the probability distribution as originally stated in Figure A.1, the variance of Asset A is 0.0005291, as shown in Figure A.11. Notice that the calculation of variance is similar to that for expected rate of return. The difference is that the expected return is subtracted from each value of rate of return and the difference is squared. Like the calculation of expected return, each one of these squared deviations is multiplied by the probability of occurrence of the appropriate state of nature.

Figure A.11 also includes a calculation of Asset A's *standard deviation*. The variance is a measure of the average squared deviation about the mean, while the standard deviation is the square root of the variance. Thus, the standard deviation is not an average squared deviation, but the absolute value of the average deviation. In the case of Asset A, the standard deviation is 0.023002, or approximately 2.3 percent. Thus, Asset A has an expected return of 6.1 percent with an average variability about that average return of 2.3 percent.

The concepts of expected return and variance are central in the decsion-making process under conditions of uncertainty. Together they approximate commonly used measures of risk and return.

Coefficient of Variation

The concepts of risk and return are combined in another measure of risk known as the *coefficient of variation*. Figure A.12 illustrates the application of this measure of risk using Asset A as an example. The coefficient of variation can be thought of as the amount of risk per unit of expected return. This measure compensates for the lack of information about variability in the expected return measure and, likewise, for the lack of information about expected return in the standard deviation.

FIGURE A.12

Coefficient of Variation, Asset A

$$CV_a = \frac{\sigma_a}{k_a{}'}$$
$$= \frac{0.023002}{0.061}$$
$$= 0.37708$$

The coefficient of variation is a ratio of risk to return, with standard deviation in the numerator and expected return in the denominator. In the case of Asset A, the units of standard deviation per unit of expected return equal 0.37708. Put another way, the coefficient of variation for Asset A suggests that for every 1 percent of expected return an investor or decision maker can expect 0.4 percent of standard deviation or risk.

RISK AND RETURN: A SUMMARY

The mathematics of uncertainty involve estimating the most likely outcome for a particular asset or scenario from a range of possible outcomes. The approach of finding the most likely outcome is also called *finding the expected return*. The expected return can be estimated using subjective probability distributions. Once the probability distribution has been determined, the expected return is the sum of all products of probabilities and the rates of return in the respective states of nature.

Alternatively, the expected return may be found by using historical data and assuming each of the past events has an equal probability of occurrence in the future. This approach of finding the expected return is a subset of the probability distribution approach in which all possible outcomes are weighted in the same manner.

While the expected return is a measure of central tendency, it is also necessary to measure variability about this central estimate – that is, the risk. Variance is the most commonly used risk measure – the most likely squared deviation about the mean or average return. The variance may be calculated assuming a subjective probability distribution that relates to the future or by using historical data as a proxy for the future. The standard deviation is the square root of the variance and is an estimate of the average deviation from the mean. Both the variance and the standard deviation measure the extent to which an outcome is likely to deviate from the measure of central tendency or average.

Another measure of risk – the coefficient of variation – incorporates the notions of both expected return and standard deviation. As the ratio of standard deviation to expected return, the coefficient of variation is risk per unit of return.

These are basic concepts in evaluating returns in a world of uncertainty. They may be incorporated into the estimate of cash flows that are applicable for capital investment and the determination of cost of capital.

PRESENT VALUE AND FUTURE VALUE FACTORS

Future Value of $1

■

Future Value of an Annuity of $1

■

Present Value of $1

■

Present Value of an Annuity of $1

Future Value of $1

$$FVIF = (1 + k)^n$$

Periods	1%	2%	3%	4%	5%	6%	7%	8%	9%	10%
1	1.0100	1.0200	1.0300	1.0400	1.0500	1.0600	1.0700	1.0800	1.0900	1.1000
2	1.0201	1.0404	1.0609	1.0816	1.1025	1.1236	1.1449	1.1664	1.1881	1.2100
3	1.0303	1.0612	1.0927	1.1249	1.1576	1.1910	1.2250	1.2597	1.2950	1.3310
4	1.0406	1.0824	1.1255	1.1699	1.2155	1.2625	1.3108	1.3605	1.4116	1.4641
5	1.0510	1.1041	1.1593	1.2167	1.2763	1.3382	1.4026	1.4693	1.5386	1.6105
6	1.0615	1.1262	1.1941	1.2653	1.3401	1.4185	1.5007	1.5869	1.6771	1.7716
7	1.0721	1.1487	1.2299	1.3159	1.4071	1.5036	1.6058	1.7138	1.8280	1.9487
8	1.0829	1.1717	1.2668	1.3686	1.4775	1.5938	1.7182	1.8509	1.9926	2.1436
9	1.0937	1.1951	1.3048	1.4233	1.5513	1.6895	1.8385	1.9990	2.1719	2.3579
10	1.1046	1.2190	1.3439	1.4802	1.6289	1.7908	1.9672	2.1589	2.3674	2.5937
11	1.1157	1.2434	1.3842	1.5395	1.7103	1.8983	2.1049	2.3316	2.5804	2.8531
12	1.1268	1.2682	1.4258	1.6010	1.7959	2.0122	2.2522	2.5182	2.8127	3.1384
13	1.1381	1.2936	1.4685	1.6651	1.8856	2.1329	2.4098	2.7196	3.0658	3.4523
14	1.1495	1.3195	1.5126	1.7317	1.9799	2.2609	2.5785	2.9372	3.3417	3.7975
15	1.1610	1.3459	1.5580	1.8009	2.0789	2.3966	2.7590	3.1722	3.6425	4.1772
16	1.1726	1.3728	1.6047	1.8730	2.1829	2.5404	2.9522	3.4259	3.9703	4.5950
17	1.1843	1.4002	1.6528	1.9479	2.2920	2.6928	3.1588	3.7000	4.3276	5.0545
18	1.1961	1.4282	1.7024	2.0258	2.4066	2.8543	3.3799	3.9960	4.7171	5.5599
19	1.2081	1.4568	1.7535	2.1068	2.5270	3.0256	3.6165	4.3157	5.1417	6.1159
20	1.2202	1.4859	1.8061	2.1911	2.6533	3.2071	3.8697	4.6610	5.6044	6.7275
25	1.2824	1.6406	2.0938	2.6658	3.3864	4.2919	5.4274	6.8485	8.6231	10.8347
30	1.3478	1.8114	2.4273	3.2434	4.3219	5.7435	7.6123	10.0627	13.2677	17.4494
35	1.4166	1.9999	2.8139	3.9461	5.5160	7.6861	10.6766	14.7853	20.4140	28.1024
40	1.4889	2.2080	3.2620	4.8010	7.0400	10.2857	14.9745	21.7245	31.4094	45.2593
45	1.5648	2.4379	3.7816	5.8412	8.9850	13.7646	21.0025	31.9204	48.3273	72.8905
50	1.6446	2.6916	4.3839	7.1067	11.4674	18.4202	29.4570	46.9016	74.3575	117.3909

Present Value And Future Value Factors

11%	12%	13%	14%	15%	16%	17%	18%	19%	20%	Periods
1.1100	1.1200	1.1300	1.1400	1.1500	1.1600	1.1700	1.1800	1.1900	1.2000	1
1.2321	1.2544	1.2769	1.2996	1.3225	1.3456	1.3689	1.3924	1.4161	1.4400	2
1.3676	1.4049	1.4429	1.4815	1.5209	1.5609	1.6016	1.6430	1.6852	1.7280	3
1.5181	1.5735	1.6305	1.6890	1.7490	1.8106	1.8739	1.9388	2.0053	2.0736	4
1.6851	1.7623	1.8424	1.9254	2.0114	2.1003	2.1924	2.2878	2.3864	2.4883	5
1.8704	1.9738	2.0820	2.1950	2.3131	2.4364	2.5652	2.6996	2.8398	2.9860	6
2.0762	2.2107	2.3526	2.5023	2.6600	2.8262	3.0012	3.1855	3.3793	3.5832	7
2.3045	2.4760	2.6584	2.8526	3.0590	3.2784	3.5115	3.7589	4.0214	4.2998	8
2.5580	2.7731	3.0040	3.2519	3.5179	3.8030	4.1084	4.4355	4.7854	5.1598	9
2.8394	3.1058	3.3946	3.7072	4.0456	4.4114	4.8068	5.2338	5.6947	6.1917	10
3.1518	3.4785	3.8359	4.2262	4.6524	5.1173	5.6240	6.1759	6.7767	7.4301	11
3.4985	3.8960	4.3345	4.8179	5.3503	5.9360	6.5801	7.2876	8.0642	8.9161	12
3.8833	4.3635	4.8980	5.4924	6.1528	6.8858	7.6987	8.5994	9.5964	10.6993	13
4.3104	4.8871	5.5348	6.2613	7.0757	7.9875	9.0075	10.1472	11.4198	12.8392	14
4.7846	5.4736	6.2543	7.1379	8.1371	9.2655	10.5387	11.9737	13.5895	15.4070	15
5.3109	6.1304	7.0673	8.1372	9.3576	10.7480	12.3303	14.1290	16.1715	18.4884	16
5.8951	6.8660	7.9861	9.2765	10.7613	12.4677	14.4265	16.6722	19.2441	22.1861	17
6.5436	7.6900	9.0243	10.5752	12.3755	14.4625	16.8790	19.6733	22.9005	26.6233	18
7.2633	8.6128	10.1974	12.0557	14.2318	16.7765	19.7484	23.2144	27.2516	31.9480	19
8.0623	9.6463	11.5231	13.7435	16.3665	19.4608	23.1056	27.3930	32.4294	38.3376	20
13.5855	17.0001	21.2305	26.4619	32.9190	40.8742	50.6578	62.6686	77.3881	95.3962	25
22.8923	29.9599	39.1159	50.9502	66.2118	85.8499	111.0647	143.3706	184.6753	237.3763	30
38.5749	52.7996	72.0685	98.1002	133.1755	180.3141	243.5035	327.9973	440.7006	590.6682	35
65.0009	93.0510	132.7816	188.8835	267.8635	378.7212	533.8687	750.3783	1.05e+03	1.47e+03	40
109.5302	163.9876	244.6414	363.6791	538.7693	795.4438	1.17e+03	1.72e+03	2.51e+03	3.66e+03	45
184.5648	289.0022	450.7359	700.2330	1.08e+03	1.67e+03	2.57e+03	3.93e+03	5.99e+03	9.10e+03	50

Future Value of an Annuity of $1

$$\text{FVIFA} = [(1 + k)^n - 1]/k$$

Periods	1%	2%	3%	4%	5%	6%	7%	8%	9%	10%
1	1.0000	1.0000	1.0000	1.0000	1.0000	1.0000	1.0000	1.0000	1.0000	1.0000
2	2.0100	2.0200	2.0300	2.0400	2.0500	2.0600	2.0700	2.0800	2.0900	2.1000
3	3.0301	3.0604	3.0909	3.1216	3.1525	3.1836	3.2149	3.2464	3.2781	3.3100
4	4.0604	4.1216	4.1836	4.2465	4.3101	4.3746	4.4399	4.5061	4.5731	4.6410
5	5.1010	5.2040	5.3091	5.4163	5.5256	5.6371	5.7507	5.8666	5.9847	6.1051
6	6.1520	6.3081	6.4684	6.6330	6.8019	6.9753	7.1533	7.3359	7.5233	7.7156
7	7.2135	7.4343	7.6625	7.8983	8.1420	8.3938	8.6540	8.9228	9.2004	9.4872
8	8.2857	8.5830	8.8923	9.2142	9.5491	9.8975	10.2598	10.6366	11.0285	11.4359
9	9.3685	9.7546	10.1591	10.5828	11.0266	11.4913	11.9780	12.4876	13.0210	13.5795
10	10.4622	10.9497	11.4639	12.0061	12.5779	13.1808	13.8164	14.4866	15.1929	15.9374
11	11.5668	12.1687	12.8078	13.4864	14.2068	14.9716	15.7836	16.6455	17.5603	18.5312
12	12.6825	13.4121	14.1920	15.0258	15.9171	16.8699	17.8885	18.9771	20.1407	21.3843
13	13.8093	14.6803	15.6178	16.6268	17.7130	18.8821	20.1406	21.4953	22.9534	24.5227
14	14.9474	15.9739	17.0863	18.2919	19.5986	21.0151	22.5505	24.2149	26.0192	27.9750
15	16.0969	17.2934	18.5989	20.0236	21.5786	23.2760	25.1290	27.1521	29.3609	31.7725
16	17.2579	18.6393	20.1569	21.8245	23.6575	25.6725	27.8881	30.3243	33.0034	35.9497
17	18.4304	20.0121	21.7616	23.6975	25.8404	28.2129	30.8402	33.7502	36.9737	40.5447
18	19.6147	21.4123	23.4144	25.6454	28.1324	30.9057	33.9990	37.4502	41.3013	45.5992
19	20.8109	22.8406	25.1169	27.6712	30.5390	33.7600	37.3790	41.4463	46.0185	51.1591
20	22.0190	24.2974	26.8704	29.7781	33.0660	36.7856	40.9955	45.7620	51.1601	57.2750
25	28.2432	32.0303	36.4593	41.6459	47.7271	54.8645	63.2490	73.1059	84.7009	98.3471
30	34.7849	40.5681	47.5754	56.0849	66.4388	79.0582	94.4608	113.2832	136.3075	164.4940
35	41.6603	49.9945	60.4621	73.6522	90.3203	111.4348	138.2369	172.3168	215.7108	271.0244
40	48.8864	60.4020	75.4013	95.0255	120.7998	154.7620	199.6351	259.0565	337.8824	442.5926
45	56.4811	71.8927	92.7199	121.0294	159.7002	212.7435	285.7493	386.5056	525.8587	718.9048
50	64.4632	84.5794	112.7969	152.6671	209.3480	290.3359	406.5289	573.7702	815.0836	1.16e+03

Present Value And Future Value Factors

11%	12%	13%	14%	15%	16%	17%	18%	19%	20%	Periods
1.0000	1.0000	1.0000	1.0000	1.0000	1.0000	1.0000	1.0000	1.0000	1.0000	1
2.1100	2.1200	2.1300	2.1400	2.1500	2.1600	2.1700	2.1800	2.1900	2.2000	2
3.3421	3.3744	3.4069	3.4396	3.4725	3.5056	3.5389	3.5724	3.6061	3.6400	3
4.7097	4.7793	4.8498	4.9211	4.9934	5.0665	5.1405	5.2154	5.2913	5.3680	4
6.2278	6.3528	6.4803	6.6101	6.7424	6.8771	7.0144	7.1542	7.2966	7.4416	5
7.9129	8.1152	8.3227	8.5355	8.7537	8.9775	9.2068	9.4420	9.6830	9.9299	6
9.7833	10.0890	10.4047	10.7305	11.0668	11.4139	11.7720	12.1415	12.5227	12.9159	7
11.8594	12.2997	12.7573	13.2328	13.7268	14.2401	14.7733	15.3270	15.9020	16.4991	8
14.1640	14.7757	15.4157	16.0853	16.7858	17.5185	18.2847	19.0859	19.9234	20.7989	9
16.7220	17.5487	18.4197	19.3373	20.3037	21.3215	22.3931	23.5213	24.7089	25.9587	10
19.5614	20.6546	21.8143	23.0445	24.3493	25.7329	27.1999	28.7551	30.4035	32.1504	11
22.7132	24.1331	25.6502	27.2707	29.0017	30.8502	32.8239	34.9311	37.1802	39.5805	12
26.2116	28.0291	29.9847	32.0887	34.3519	36.7862	39.4040	42.2187	45.2445	48.4966	13
30.0949	32.3926	34.8827	37.5811	40.5047	43.6720	47.1027	50.8180	54.8409	59.1959	14
34.4054	37.2797	40.4175	43.8424	47.5804	51.6595	56.1101	60.9653	66.2607	72.0351	15
39.1899	42.7533	46.6717	50.9804	55.7175	60.9250	66.6488	72.9390	79.8502	87.4421	16
44.5008	48.8837	53.7391	59.1176	65.0751	71.6730	78.9792	87.0680	96.0218	105.9306	17
50.3959	55.7497	61.7251	68.3941	75.8364	84.1407	93.4056	103.7403	115.2659	128.1167	18
56.9395	63.4397	70.7494	78.9692	88.2118	98.6032	110.2846	123.4135	138.1664	154.7400	19
64.2028	72.0524	80.9468	91.0249	102.4436	115.3797	130.0329	146.6280	165.4180	186.6880	20
114.4133	133.3339	155.6196	181.8708	212.7930	249.2140	292.1049	342.6035	402.0425	471.9811	25
199.0209	241.3327	293.1992	356.7868	434.7451	530.3117	647.4391	790.9480	966.7122	1.18e+03	30
341.5896	431.6635	546.6808	693.5727	881.1702	1.12e+03	1.43e+03	1.82e+03	2.31e+03	2.95e+03	35
581.8261	767.0914	1.01e+03	1.34e+03	1.78e+03	2.36e+03	3.13e+03	4.16e+03	5.53e+03	7.34e+03	40
986.6386	1.36e+03	1.87e+03	2.59e+03	3.59e+03	4.97e+03	6.88e+03	9.53e+03	1.32e+04	1.83e+04	45
1.67e+03	2.40e+03	3.46e+03	4.99e+03	7.22e+03	1.04e+04	1.51e+04	2.18e+04	3.15e+04	4.55e+04	50

Present Value of $1

$$PVIF = 1/(1+k)^n$$

Periods	1%	2%	3%	4%	5%	6%	7%	8%	9%	10%
1	0.9901	0.9804	0.9709	0.9615	0.9524	0.9434	0.9346	0.9259	0.9174	0.9091
2	0.9803	0.9612	0.9426	0.9246	0.9070	0.8900	0.8734	0.8573	0.8417	0.8264
3	0.9706	0.9423	0.9151	0.8890	0.8638	0.8396	0.8163	0.7938	0.7722	0.7513
4	0.9610	0.9238	0.8885	0.8548	0.8227	0.7921	0.7629	0.7350	0.7084	0.6830
5	0.9515	0.9057	0.8626	0.8219	0.7835	0.7473	0.7130	0.6806	0.6499	0.6209
6	0.9420	0.8880	0.8375	0.7903	0.7462	0.7050	0.6663	0.6302	0.5963	0.5645
7	0.9327	0.8706	0.8131	0.7599	0.7107	0.6651	0.6227	0.5835	0.5470	0.5132
8	0.9235	0.8535	0.7894	0.7307	0.6768	0.6274	0.5820	0.5403	0.5019	0.4665
9	0.9143	0.8368	0.7664	0.7026	0.6446	0.5919	0.5439	0.5002	0.4604	0.4241
10	0.9053	0.8203	0.7441	0.6756	0.6139	0.5584	0.5083	0.4632	0.4224	0.3855
11	0.8963	0.8043	0.7224	0.6496	0.5847	0.5268	0.4751	0.4289	0.3875	0.3505
12	0.8874	0.7885	0.7014	0.6246	0.5568	0.4970	0.4440	0.3971	0.3555	0.3186
13	0.8787	0.7730	0.6810	0.6006	0.5303	0.4688	0.4150	0.3677	0.3262	0.2897
14	0.8700	0.7579	0.6611	0.5775	0.5051	0.4423	0.3878	0.3405	0.2992	0.2633
15	0.8613	0.7430	0.6419	0.5553	0.4810	0.4173	0.3624	0.3152	0.2745	0.2394
16	0.8528	0.7284	0.6232	0.5339	0.4581	0.3936	0.3387	0.2919	0.2519	0.2176
17	0.8444	0.7142	0.6050	0.5134	0.4363	0.3714	0.3166	0.2703	0.2311	0.1978
18	0.8360	0.7002	0.5874	0.4936	0.4155	0.3503	0.2959	0.2502	0.2120	0.1799
19	0.8277	0.6864	0.5703	0.4746	0.3957	0.3305	0.2765	0.2317	0.1945	0.1635
20	0.8195	0.6730	0.5537	0.4564	0.3769	0.3118	0.2584	0.2145	0.1784	0.1486
25	0.7798	0.6095	0.4776	0.3751	0.2953	0.2330	0.1842	0.1460	0.1160	0.0923
30	0.7419	0.5521	0.4120	0.3083	0.2314	0.1741	0.1314	0.0994	0.0754	0.0573
35	0.7059	0.5000	0.3554	0.2534	0.1813	0.1301	0.0937	0.0676	0.0490	0.0356
40	0.6717	0.4529	0.3066	0.2083	0.1420	0.0972	0.0668	0.0460	0.0318	0.0221
45	0.6391	0.4102	0.2644	0.1712	0.1113	0.0727	0.0476	0.0313	0.0207	0.0137
50	1.0000	0.3715	0.2281	0.1407	0.0872	0.0543	0.0339	0.0213	0.0134	0.0085

Present Value And Future Value Factors

11%	12%	13%	14%	15%	16%	17%	18%	19%	20%	Periods
0.9009	0.8929	0.8850	0.8772	0.8696	0.8621	0.8547	0.8475	0.8403	0.8333	1
0.8116	0.7972	0.7831	0.7695	0.7561	0.7432	0.7305	0.7182	0.7062	0.6944	2
0.7312	0.7118	0.6931	0.6750	0.6575	0.6407	0.6244	0.6086	0.5934	0.5787	3
0.6587	0.6355	0.6133	0.5921	0.5718	0.5523	0.5337	0.5158	0.4987	0.4823	4
0.5935	0.5674	0.5428	0.5194	0.4972	0.4761	0.4561	0.4371	0.4190	0.4019	5
0.5346	0.5066	0.4803	0.4556	0.4323	0.4104	0.3898	0.3704	0.3521	0.3349	6
0.4817	0.4523	0.4251	0.3996	0.3759	0.3538	0.3332	0.3139	0.2959	0.2791	7
0.4339	0.4039	0.3762	0.3506	0.3269	0.3050	0.2848	0.2660	0.2487	0.2326	8
0.3909	0.3606	0.3329	0.3075	0.2843	0.2630	0.2434	0.2255	0.2090	0.1938	9
0.3522	0.3220	0.2946	0.2697	0.2472	0.2267	0.2080	0.1911	0.1756	0.1615	10
0.3173	0.2875	0.2607	0.2366	0.2149	0.1954	0.1778	0.1619	0.1476	0.1346	11
0.2858	0.2567	0.2307	0.2076	0.1869	0.1685	0.1520	0.1372	0.1240	0.1122	12
0.2575	0.2292	0.2042	0.1821	0.1625	0.1452	0.1299	0.1163	0.1042	0.0935	13
0.2320	0.2046	0.1807	0.1597	0.1413	0.1252	0.1110	0.0985	0.0876	0.0779	14
0.2090	0.1827	0.1599	0.1401	0.1229	0.1079	0.0949	0.0835	0.0736	0.0649	15
0.1883	0.1631	0.1415	0.1229	0.1069	0.0930	0.0811	0.0708	0.0618	0.0541	16
0.1696	0.1456	0.1252	0.1078	0.0929	0.0802	0.0693	0.0600	0.0520	0.0451	17
0.1528	0.1300	0.1108	0.0946	0.0808	0.0691	0.0592	0.0508	0.0437	0.0376	18
0.1377	0.1161	0.0981	0.0829	0.0703	0.0596	0.0506	0.0431	0.0367	0.0313	19
0.1240	0.1037	0.0868	0.0728	0.0611	0.0514	0.0433	0.0365	0.0308	0.0261	20
0.0736	0.0588	0.0471	0.0378	0.0304	0.0245	0.0197	0.0160	0.0129	0.0105	25
0.0437	0.0334	0.0256	0.0196	0.0151	0.0116	0.0090	0.0070	0.0054	0.0042	30
0.0259	0.0189	0.0139	0.0102	0.0075	0.0055	0.0041	0.0030	0.0023	0.0017	35
0.0154	0.0107	0.0075	0.0053	0.0037	0.0026	0.0019	0.0013	0.0010	0.0007	40
0.0091	0.0061	0.0041	0.0027	0.0019	0.0013	0.0009	0.0006	0.0004	0.0003	45
0.0054	0.0035	0.0022	0.0014	0.0009	0.0006	0.0004	0.0003	0.0002	0.0001	50

Present Value of an Annuity of $1

$$PVIFA = [1-1/(1+k)^n]/k$$

Periods	1%	2%	3%	4%	5%	6%	7%	8%	9%	10%
1	0.9901	0.9804	0.9709	0.9615	0.9524	0.9434	0.9346	0.9259	0.9174	0.9091
2	1.9704	1.9416	1.9135	1.8861	1.8594	1.8334	1.8080	1.7833	1.7591	1.7355
3	2.9410	2.8839	2.8286	2.7751	2.7232	2.6730	2.6243	2.5771	2.5313	2.4869
4	3.9020	3.8077	3.7171	3.6299	3.5460	3.4651	3.3872	3.3121	3.2397	3.1699
5	4.8534	4.7135	4.5797	4.4518	4.3295	4.2124	4.1002	3.9927	3.8897	3.7908
6	5.7955	5.6014	5.4172	5.2421	5.0757	4.9173	4.7665	4.6229	4.4859	4.3553
7	6.7282	6.4720	6.2303	6.0021	5.7864	5.5824	5.3893	5.2064	5.0330	4.8684
8	7.6517	7.3255	7.0197	6.7327	6.4632	6.2098	5.9713	5.7466	5.5348	5.3349
9	8.5660	8.1622	7.7861	7.4353	7.1078	6.8017	6.5152	6.2469	5.9952	5.7590
10	9.4713	8.9826	8.5302	8.1109	7.7217	7.3601	7.0236	6.7101	6.4177	6.1446
11	10.3676	9.7868	9.2526	8.7605	8.3064	7.8869	7.4987	7.1390	6.8052	6.4951
12	11.2551	10.5753	9.9540	9.3851	8.8633	8.3838	7.9427	7.5361	7.1607	6.8137
13	12.1337	11.3484	10.6350	9.9856	9.3936	8.8527	8.3577	7.9038	7.4869	7.1034
14	13.0037	12.1062	11.2961	10.5631	9.8986	9.2950	8.7455	8.2442	7.7862	7.3667
15	13.8651	12.8493	11.9379	11.1184	10.3797	9.7122	9.1079	8.5595	8.0607	7.6061
16	14.7179	13.5777	12.5611	11.6523	10.8378	10.1059	9.4466	8.8514	8.3126	7.8237
17	15.5623	14.2919	13.1661	12.1657	11.2741	10.4773	9.7632	9.1216	8.5436	8.0216
18	16.3983	14.9920	13.7535	12.6593	11.6896	10.8276	10.0591	9.3719	8.7556	8.2014
19	17.2260	15.6785	14.3238	13.1339	12.0853	11.1581	10.3356	9.6036	8.9501	8.3649
20	18.0456	16.3514	14.8775	13.5903	12.4622	11.4699	10.5940	9.8181	9.1285	8.5136
25	22.0232	19.5235	17.4131	15.6221	14.0939	12.7834	11.6536	10.6748	9.8226	9.0770
30	25.8077	22.3965	19.6004	17.2920	15.3725	13.7648	12.4090	11.2578	10.2737	9.4269
35	29.4086	24.9986	21.4872	18.6646	16.3742	14.4982	12.9477	11.6546	10.5668	9.6442
40	32.8347	27.3555	23.1148	19.7928	17.1591	15.0463	13.3317	11.9246	10.7574	9.7791
45	36.0945	29.4902	24.5187	20.7200	17.7741	15.4558	13.6055	12.1084	10.8812	9.8628
50	39.1961	31.4236	25.7298	21.4822	18.2559	15.7619	13.8007	12.2335	10.9617	9.9148

Present Value And Future Value Factors

11%	12%	13%	14%	15%	16%	17%	18%	19%	20%	Periods
0.9009	0.8929	0.8850	0.8772	0.8696	0.8621	0.8547	0.8475	0.8403	0.8333	1
1.7125	1.6901	1.6681	1.6467	1.6257	1.6052	1.5852	1.5656	1.5465	1.5278	2
2.4437	2.4018	2.3612	2.3216	2.2832	2.2459	2.2096	2.1743	2.1399	2.1065	3
3.1024	3.0373	2.9745	2.9137	2.8550	2.7982	2.7432	2.6901	2.6386	2.5887	4
3.6959	3.6048	3.5172	3.4331	3.3522	3.2743	3.1993	3.1272	3.0576	2.9906	5
4.2305	4.1114	3.9975	3.8887	3.7845	3.6847	3.5892	3.4976	3.4098	3.3255	6
4.7122	4.5638	4.4226	4.2883	4.1604	4.0386	3.9224	3.8115	3.7057	3.6046	7
5.1461	4.9676	4.7988	4.6389	4.4873	4.3436	4.2072	4.0776	3.9544	3.8372	8
5.5370	5.3282	5.1317	4.9464	4.7716	4.6065	4.4506	4.3030	4.1633	4.0310	9
5.8892	5.6502	5.4262	5.2161	5.0188	4.8332	4.6586	4.4941	4.3389	4.1925	10
6.2065	5.9377	5.6869	5.4527	5.2337	5.0286	4.8364	4.6560	4.4865	4.3271	11
6.4924	6.1944	5.9176	5.6603	5.4206	5.1971	4.9884	4.7932	4.6105	4.4392	12
6.7499	6.4235	6.1218	5.8424	5.5831	5.3423	5.1183	4.9095	4.7147	4.5327	13
6.9819	6.6282	6.3025	6.0021	5.7245	5.4675	5.2293	5.0081	4.8023	4.6106	14
7.1909	6.8109	6.4624	6.1422	5.8474	5.5755	5.3242	5.0916	4.8759	4.6755	15
7.3792	6.9740	6.6039	6.2651	5.9542	5.6685	5.4053	5.1624	4.9377	4.7296	16
7.5488	7.1196	6.7291	6.3729	6.0472	5.7487	5.4746	5.2223	4.9897	4.7746	17
7.7016	7.2497	6.8399	6.4674	6.1280	5.8178	5.5339	5.2732	5.0333	4.8122	18
7.8393	7.3658	6.9380	6.5504	6.1982	5.8775	5.5845	5.3162	5.0700	4.8435	19
7.9633	7.4694	7.0248	6.6231	6.2593	5.9288	5.6278	5.3527	5.1009	4.8696	20
8.4217	7.8431	7.3300	6.8729	6.4641	6.0971	5.7662	5.4669	5.1951	4.9476	25
8.6938	8.0552	7.4957	7.0027	6.5660	6.1772	5.8294	5.5168	5.2347	4.9789	30
8.8552	8.1755	7.5856	7.0700	6.6166	6.2153	5.8582	5.5386	5.2512	4.9915	35
8.9511	8.2438	7.6344	7.1050	6.6418	6.2335	5.8713	5.5482	5.2582	4.9966	40
9.0079	8.2825	7.6609	7.1232	6.6543	6.2421	5.8773	5.5523	5.2611	4.9986	45
9.0417	8.3045	7.6752	7.1327	6.6605	6.2463	5.8801	5.5541	5.2623	4.9995	50

COST OF EQUITY OF A PRIVATELY HELD FIRM

Capital Asset Pricing Model

■

Beta of Assets and Equity

■

Example of a Single Industry

■

Example of Multiple Industries

CAPITAL ASSET PRICING MODEL

As explained in Chapter 5, the Capital Asset Pricing Model (CAPM) associates cost of capital with volatility of returns. A project with highly variable cash flows will have a high *beta* and, accordingly, a high cost of capital. In this context, beta is a measure of overall asset variability as compared to the market portfolio.

CAPM is also appropriate to estimate the *cost of equity* in the *weighted average cost of capital* (WACC). In this case, beta is a measure of equity return variability.

$$k_E = k_{rf} + \beta_E (k_m - k_{rf})$$

where k_E = cost of equity

k_{rf} = risk-free rate

= return on Treasury

β_E = beta of equity

k_m = return of the market portfolio

= return on a stock index

The *ß of the equity* is related to the *ß of the assets* and the firm's *debt-to-equity ratio*.

$$\beta_E = \beta_A \left(1 + \frac{D}{E} \right)$$

where β_A = beta of the assets

$\dfrac{D}{E}$ = debt-to-equity ratio

Solving for β_A:

$$\frac{\beta_E}{\left(1 + \dfrac{D}{E} \right)} = \beta_A$$

BETA OF ASSETS AND EQUITY

When stock is *not publicly traded*, the cost of equity can be approximated by the following five steps:

- Use external data sources to determine the appropriate industry code. The Standard Industrial Code (SIC) system is used in the USA. The Standard International Trade Classification (SITC) system has been adopted by the United Nations. The SIC or SITC is used to determine an *industry debt-to-equity ratio*. If more than one SIC is appropriate, determine the industry debt-to-equity ratio for each.
- Use external data to determine β_E *for the industry*.[1]
- Use the equation above to estimate the β_A *for the industry*. If the firm is engaged in more than one industry, determine the weighted average of the industry β_As.
- Calculate the β_E.
- Calculate the *cost of equity*.

EXAMPLE OF A SINGLE INDUSTRY

To illustrate the use of CAPM for a privately held firm, assume:

- SIC is associated with an industry debt-to-equity ratio of **1.90**.
- *β* of the industry equity is **2.0**.
- The firm's debt-to-equity ratio is **6.70**.
- Risk-free rate is **6.5 percent**.
- Return on a broad-based market index is **11.0 percent**.

Beta of industry assets is **0.6897**:

$$\frac{2.0}{(1 + 1.9)} = \beta_A = 0.6897$$

---

[1] Betas are calculated by a number of firms, for example, Value Line in the USA.

Beta of equity is **5.31**.

$$\beta_E = 0.6897(1 + 6.70)$$
$$= 5.31$$

The cost of equity is **30.395 percent**.

$$k_E = 0.065 + 5.31(0.11 - 0.065)$$
$$= 0.30395$$
$$= 30.395\%$$

EXAMPLE OF MULTIPLE INDUSTRIES

In this example, assume:

- The firm has three SICs and the mix of business is as shown in Figure C.1.
- The debt-to-equity ratio is **5.38**.
- Risk-free rate is **6.5 percent**.
- Return on a broad-based market index is **11.0 percent**.

Based on these assumptions:

Betas of industry assets for the three SICs are **0.6875**, **0.71875**, and **0.6897**, respectively.

FIGURE C.1			
Mix of Business			
SIC	Industry β_E	Industry D/E	% of Business for firm
1	2.2	2.2	50%
2	2.3	2.2	40%
3	2.0	1.9	10%

For SIC 1:

$$\frac{2.2}{(1 + 2.2)} = \beta_A = 0.6875$$

For SIC 2:

$$\frac{2.3}{(1 + 2.2)} = \beta_A = 0.71875$$

For SIC 3:

$$\frac{2.0}{(1 + 1.9)} = \beta_A = 0.6897$$

The weighted average β of the assets is **0.70022**.

$$\begin{aligned} \beta_A &= 0.50(0.6875) + 0.40(0.71875) + 0.10(0.6897) \\ &= 0.34375 + 0.2875 + 0.06897 \\ &= 0.70022 \end{aligned}$$

Beta of equity is **4.47**.

$$\begin{aligned} \beta_E &= 0.70022 \, (1 + 5.38) \\ &= 4.47 \end{aligned}$$

The cost of equity is **26.615 percent**.

$$\begin{aligned} k_E &= 0.065 + 4.47(0.11 - 0.065) \\ &= 0.26615 \\ &= 26.615\% \end{aligned}$$

INDEX

COST OF CAPITAL SOFTWARE SYSTEM
(INTERACTIVE VERSION)

© Hazel J. Johnson 1999
Software Development Consultant: Derrick M. Johnson

Introduction

Cost of Capital Software System is an Excel 7.0-based system that provides a framework in which to determine the cost of capital for:

- a company whose common stock is publicly traded (COC_PUB.xls);
- a company whose common stock is privately held (COC_PRIV.xls).

The system is organized in a workbook format. Individual worksheets address the individual components of the cost of capital.

Name of Worksheet	Publicly Held	Privately Held
Cost of Debt	Yes	Yes
Cost of Preferred Stock	Yes	Yes
Beta of Equity	Yes	Yes
Market Returns	n/a	Yes
Cost of Equity	Yes	Yes
Weighted Average Cost of Capital	Yes	Yes

Each worksheet requires input from the user as indicated by a cell address in parentheses. For example,

Tax rate – decimal (D37)

means that the user should place the tax rate in decimal form in cell D37.

Other line items are accompanied with the phrase (*do not input*). In these cases, the system is programmed to produce the result. No user input is required.

The following pages explain each individual worksheet.

USER'S MANUAL

System Installation

To install *Cost of Capital Software System*, save Coc_Pub.xls and Coc_Priv.xls on a hard drive with at least 500 kb of available disk space.

The *Cost of Capital Software System* should be placed on the user's hard drive. In this way, should any of the code be erased inadvertently, the diskette version of the program can be used to reinstall the system.

System Operation

On the Windows task bar, press "Start" button. Choose "run." In the dialogue box, type the full path name of the file, for example,

c:\coc\coc_pub.xls

where c:\coc is the path of the file. The first worksheet will appear – "Cost_of_Debt."

Manual Mode

To use the system as a regular spreadsheet, in "Cost_of_Debt," input for each category of debt, the account name (type) in column A and the corresponding information requested in columns D, E, and F for the account type. Use rows 11 through 34, as necessary, to record all applicable debt categories. Lastly, enter the firm's marginal income tax rate in decimal form in cell D37. Continue this process through the following sheets:

- Cost_of_Preferred
- Beta_of_Equity
- Market_Returns (privately held firm only)
- Cost_of_Equity
- WACC.

Interactive Mode

Click "Main Menu" button on "Cost_of_Debt" worksheet.

- To analyze each component of capital:
  - select "Interactive Mode;"
  - press the "Next" button;
  - enter the account name (type), total book value of this type of debt, total market value of this type of debt, and the component cost (cost of debt) in decimal form;
  - use the tab key to move from one text box to the subsequent text box (for example, from "account name" to "book value of debt" and then to "market value of debt");
  - press "Next" button or press Enter to proceed to the next debt category. Continue the input as requested;
  - up to 24 categories of debt may be used. If less than 24 categories are required, the "Next Sheet" button will select the subsequent worksheet that requires input;
  - after pressing "Next Sheet" but before moving to the subsequent worksheet, the user will be asked whether the remaining rows should be cleared. If "yes" is selected, all entries in the rows below the current row (columns A, D, E, and F) of Cost_of_Debt will be deleted. If "no" is selected, subsequent entries in these columns will remain intact;
  - the "Exit" button will terminate the Interactive Mode and place the cursor in the last field of input.
- To return to the Manual Mode, select "Manual Mode" and press "Next." The following sections describe the specific data required in each case.

Cost of Debt

This worksheet permits the user to record the components of debt and the cost associated with each. Categories are included for the purposes of organization. However, the category titles – bank notes, revolving credit, bonds, and other long-term debt – have no impact on the calculations. Any row between 11 and 34 may be used for any classification of long-term debt.

It is assumed that both publicly traded and privately held firms may have publicly traded debt. Accordingly, the following data are required for type of long-term debt:

- Total book value
- Total market value
- Component cost, that is, rate of interest on debt in decimal form.

If debt is not publicly traded, market value will equal book value.

The user must provide a tax rate in cell D37 – the marginal income tax rate. In manual mode, input of the tax rate is in cell D37. In interactive mode, the tax rate is input in the first long-term debt category (account 1 of 24).

The system automatically computes the total book value and total market value, market weight (percentage of total market value represented by each component of debt), pre-tax weighted cost of debt, and after-tax cost of debt.

Cost of Preferred Stock

The user should input total book value of preferred stock, number of shares outstanding, market value per share, and dividend per share. Again, it is assumed that privately held firms may have publicly traded preferred stock. If preferred stock is not publicly traded, market value will equal book value.

The system automatically calculates total market value and component cost, that is, the cost of preferred stock.

If the user has no preferred stock outstanding, zeros can be input in the appropriate cells (manual mode) or text boxes (interactive mode).

Beta of Equity – Public Firm

For a publicly held firm, the beta of equity will be (1) the covariance of returns of the stock with returns of the market divided by (2) the variance of market returns. The system computes these statistics and the resulting beta.

The user should input stock prices for 61 consecutive month-ends or the number of consecutive month-ends for which stock prices are available (if the stock has not traded publicly for the entire five-year period). For the same month-ends, the user should input the values of a broad-based stock index in the same country in which the stock is traded.

204

If both stock price and index value are not present for a particular month, the results will not be computed.

Manual Mode

In manual mode, month-end stock prices are input in column B. The corresponding index values are input in column C. The user should delete contents in unused rows of columns B and C.

Interactive Mode

In interactive mode, the user is asked to input the stock price and index value for each of the 61 month-end sets of stock price and index value. If less than 61 sets of values are available, the user may leave the Beta_of_Equity worksheet by pressing "Next Sheet." After pressing "Next Sheet" but before moving to the subsequent worksheet, the user will be asked whether the remaining rows should be cleared. If "yes" is selected, all entries in the rows below the current row (columns B and C) will be deleted. If "no" is selected, the subsequent entries in Beta_of_Equity will remain intact.

Beta of Equity – Privately Held Firm

For the privately held firm, the beta of equity depends on data concerning the industry in which the firm operates:

- Beta of the industry
- Debt-equity ratio of industry
- Percentage of the firm's total business as measured in revenues or assets in the industry.

This is repeated for each industry in which the firm operates.

The system automatically computes the beta of assets in each industry and the weighted average beta of assets for the firm.

The user then inputs the debt-equity ratio for the firm. In manual mode, the debt-equity ratio of the firm is input in cell E35. The system automatically calculates the beta of equity.

Market Returns – Privately Held Firm

This worksheet computes an expected return for the market in order to use CAPM. The user inputs the values of a broad-based stock index for 61 consecutive months. The system automatically computes the expected return for the number of months that have been input.

Manual Mode

In manual mode, month-end index values are input in column C. The user should delete contents of unused rows in column C of Market_Returns.

Interactive Mode

In interactive mode, the user is asked to input the index value for each of 61 month-ends. If less than 61 values are available, the user may leave the Market_Returns worksheet by pressing "Next Sheet." After pressing "Next Sheet" but before moving to the subsequent worksheet, the user will be asked whether the remaining rows should be cleared. If "yes" is selected, all entries in the rows below the current row (column C) will be deleted. If "No" is selected, the subsequent entries in Market_Returns will remain intact.

Cost of Equity – Public Firm

The user need input only the annual risk-free interest rate in decimal form and the amount of minority interest in subsidiary(ies). In manual mode, these inputs are in cells F7 and F35, respectively.

The system automatically calculates the average of (1) the CAPM result and (2) the average annual capital gain or loss on the stock. This result is the cost of equity.

Cost of Equity – Privately Held Firm

The user need input only the annual risk-free interest rate in decimal form and the amount of minority interest in subsidiary(ies). In manual mode, these inputs are in cells F7 and F20, respectively.

The cost of equity is automatically calculated using the CAPM approach.

Weighted Average Cost of Capital

With selected input from the user in terms of book value of common equity, number of common shares outstanding, and market value per share of common shares outstanding (publicly held only), the system automatically calculates the weighted average cost of capital as the total of the weighted cost column.